A Life's Work

On Becoming a Mother

RACHEL CUSK

Picador
New York

For Adrian

A LIFE'S WORK. Copyright © 2001 by Rachel Cusk. All rights reserved. Printed in the United States of America. No part of this book may be used or reproduced in any manner whatsoever without written permission except in the case of brief quotations embodied in critical articles or reviews. For information, address Picador, 120 Broadway, New York, N.Y. 10271.

Picador® is a U.S. registered trademark and is used by Macmillan Publishing Group, LLC, under license from Pan Books Limited.

picadorusa.com • instagram.com/picador
twitter.com/picadorusa • facebook.com/picadorusa

For book club information, please visit facebook.com/picadorbookclub or e-mail marketing@picadorusa.com.

Library of Congress Cataloging-in-Publication Data

Cusk, Rachel.
    A life's work : on becoming a mother / Rachel Cusk.
        p. cm.
    ISBN 0-312-26987-0 (hc)
    ISBN 0-312-31130-3 (pbk)
    1. Motherhood. 2. Parenting. I. Title.
HQ759 .C985 2002
306.874'—dc21   2001054894

First published in Great Britain by Fourth Estate,
a division of HarperCollins*Publishers*

First Picador Paperback Edition: March 2003

D10 9 8 7 6 5 4 3

Acknowledgements

I wish to thank Reagan Arthur and Georgia Garrett, for many deeply felt conversations and communications on the subject of motherhood. My stepdaughter, friend and ultimate ally Molly Clarke is an unspoken presence in these pages: I hope that one day she will read them and like them. She may not remember the dark February night on which she gave me her lucky necklace, but I do.

As child is equivalent with imagination, the mother's language becomes unimaginative, imperative, abstract. As the child is growth, she becomes static and empty, unable to react with spontaneous novelty. As the child is timeless, eternal, she becomes time-bound, scheduled, hurried. Her morality becomes one-sidedly responsible and disciplinarian. Her sense of future and hope is displaced on her actual child; thereby postpartum depression may become a chronic undertone. As her actual child carries her feelings of vulnerability, she may over-attend to it to the neglect of herself, with consequent resentments. Also, her thought processes become restricted to adult forms of reason so that the ghost voices and faces, animals, the scenes of eidectic imagination become estranged and feel like pathological delusions and hallucinations. And her language loses its emotion and incantational power; she explains and argues.

James Hillman, 'The Bad Mother'

Contents

Introduction

If at any point in my life I had been able to find out what the future held, I would always have wanted to know whether or not I would have children. More than love, more than work, more than length of life or quantity of happiness, this was the question whose mystery I found most compelling. I could imagine those other things; giving birth to a child I could not. I wanted to know whether I would go through it, not because this knowledge would have made motherhood imaginable, but because it seemed to me that the issue could not remain shrouded in uncertainty without becoming a distraction. It was this distraction, as much as the fact of motherhood itself, that I wanted to have within my control. I regarded it as a threat, a form of disability that marked me out as unequal. But women must and do live with the prospect of childbirth: some dread it, some long for it, and some manage it so successfully as to give other people the impression that they never even think about it. My own strategy was to deny it,

I

and so I arrived at the fact of motherhood shocked and unprepared, ignorant of what the consequences of this arrival would be, and with the unfounded but distinct impression that my journey there had been at once so random and so determined by forces greater than myself that I could hardly be said to have had any choice in the matter at all.

This book is an attempt to describe something of that arrival, and of the drama of which childbirth is merely the opening scene. It is, necessarily, a personal record of a period of transition. My desire to express myself on the subject of motherhood was from the beginning strong, but it dwelt underground, beneath the reconfigured surface of my life. A few months after the birth of my daughter Albertine, it vanished entirely. I wilfully forgot everything that I had felt so keenly, so little time ago: I couldn't bear, in fact, to feel it. My appetite for the world was insatiable, omnivorous, an expression of longing for some lost, pre-maternal self, and for the freedom that self had perhaps enjoyed, perhaps squandered. Motherhood, for me, was a sort of compound fenced off from the rest of the world. I was forever plotting my escape from it, and when I found myself pregnant again when Albertine was six months old I greeted my old cell with the cheerless acceptance of a convict intercepted at large. What I had begun cautiously to think of as freedom became an exiguous hammock slung between the trunks of two pregnancies: I was surrounded,

2

and it was then that the strange reality of motherhood grew apparent to me once more. I wrote this book during the pregnancy and early months of my second daughter, Jessye, before it could get away again.

I make this explanation with the gloomy suspicion that a book about motherhood is of no real interest to anyone except other mothers; and even then only mothers who, like me, find the experience so momentous that reading about it has a strangely narcotic effect. I say 'other mothers' and 'only mothers' as if in apology: the experience of motherhood loses nearly everything in its translation to the outside world. In motherhood a woman exchanges her public significance for a range of private meanings, and like sounds outside a certain range they can be very difficult for other people to identify. If one listened with a different part of oneself, one would perhaps hear them. 'All human life on the planet is born of woman,' wrote the American poet and feminist Adrienne Rich. 'The one unifying, incontrovertible experience shared by all women and men is that months-long period we spent unfolding inside a woman's body . . . Most of us first know both love and disappointment, power and tenderness, in the person of a woman. We carry the imprint of this experience for life, even into our dying.'

There are, of course, many important analyses, histories, polemics and social studies of motherhood. It has been seriously examined as an issue of class, of geography, of politics, of race, of psychology. In 1977 Adrienne Rich wrote the seminal *Of Woman Born: Motherhood as Institution and Experience*, and it is inspired by her example that I offer my own account. Yet it was my impression, when I became a mother, that nothing had been written about it at all: this may merely be a good example of that tone-deafness I describe, with which a non-parent is afflicted whenever a parent speaks, a condition we acquire as children and which leads us as adults to wonder in bemusement why we were never told – by our friends, *by our mothers!* – what parenthood was like. I am certain that my own reaction, three years ago, to the book I have now written would have been to wonder why the author had bothered to have children in the first place if she thought it was so awful.

This is not a history or study of motherhood; nor, in case anyone has read this far and still retains such a hope, is it a book about how to be a mother. I have merely written down what I thought of the experience of having a child in a way that I hope other people can identify with. As a novelist, I admit that I find this candid type of writing slightly alarming. Aside from the prospect of self-revelation, it demands on the part of the author a willingness to trespass on the lives of those around him or her. In this case, I have trespassed by omission. I have not said much about my particular circumstances, nor about the people with whom I live, nor about the other relationships inevitably surrounding the relationship I describe with my child. Instead I have used aspects of my life as a canvas upon which my theme, which is motherhood, may conveniently be illustrated.

But the issue of children and who looks after them has become, in my view, profoundly political, and so it would be a contradiction to write a book about motherhood without explaining to some degree how I found the time to write it. For the first six months of Albertine's life I looked after her at home while my partner continued to work. This experience forcefully revealed to me something to which I had never given much thought: the fact that after a child is born the lives of its mother and father diverge, so that where before they were living in a state of some equality, now they exist in a sort of feudal relation to each other. A day spent at home caring for a child could not be more different from a day spent working in an office. Whatever their relative merits, they are days spent on opposite sides of the world. From that irreconcilable beginning, it seemed to me that some kind of slide into deeper patriarchy was inevitable: that the father's day would gradually gather to it the armour of the outside world, of money and authority and impor- tance, while the mother's remit would extend to cover the entire domestic sphere. It is well known that in couples where both parents work full-time, the mother generally does far more than her fair share of housework and childcare, and is the one to curtail her working day in order to meet the exigencies of parenthood. That is an issue of sexual politics; but even in the most generous household, which I acknowledge my own to be, the gulf between childcarer and worker is profound. Bridging it is extremely difficult. It is one solution for the father to remain at home while the mother works: in our culture, the male and the female remain so divided, so embedded in conservatism, that a man could perhaps look after children without feeling that he was his partner's servant. Few men, however, would countenance the injury to their career that such a course would invite; those who would are by implication more committed than most to equality, and risk the same loss of self-esteem that makes a career in motherhood such a difficult prospect for women. Both parents can work and employ a nanny or childminder, or sometimes each can work a shorter week and spend some days at home and some at work. This is rather more difficult if one of you works at home, in spite of the widely held belief that a career such as my own is 'ideal' if you have children. An unfair apportioning of domestic responsibility to the home worker is unavoidable. Their role begins to resemble that of an air traffic controller.

Full-time paid childcare was what I, with the blithe unsentimentality of the childless, once believed to be the solution to the conundrum of work and motherhood. In those days fairness seemed to me to be everything. I did not understand what a challenge to the concept of sexual equality the experience of pregnancy and childbirth is. Birth is not merely that which divides women from men: it also divides women from themselves, so that a woman's understanding of what it is to exist is profoundly changed. Another person has existed in her, and after their birth they live within the jurisdiction of her consciousness. When she is with them she is not herself; when she is without them she is not herself; and so it is as difficult to leave your children as it is to stay with them. To discover this is to feel that your life has become irretrievably mired in conflict, or caught in some mythic snare in which you will perpetually, vainly struggle.

In my case a decision was made to demolish traditional family culture altogether, and it was regarded by other people with amazement, approval and horror. The most punitive, unworkable version of family life appears to be less worthy of general comment and concern than simple unconventionality. My partner left his job and we moved out of London. People began to enquire about him as if he were very ill, or dead. What's he going to *do*? they would ask me avidly, and then, getting no answer, him. Look after the children while Rachel writes her book about looking after the children, was his reply. Nobody else seemed to find this particularly funny.

Looking after children is a low-status occupation. It is isolating, frequently boring, relentlessly demanding and exhausting. It erodes your self-esteem and your membership of the adult world. The more it is separated from the rest of life, the harder it gets; and yet to bring your children to your own existence, rather than move yourself to theirs, is hard too. Even when you agree on a version of living that is acceptable to everybody, there are still longings that go unmet. It is my belief that in this enterprise generosity is more important even than equality, if only because the demonology of parenthood is so catholic, drawing to itself epithets of 'good' and 'bad' that are largely absent from our experience of ordinary life. As a mother you learn what it is to be both martyr and devil. In motherhood I have experienced myself as both more virtuous and more terrible, and more implicated too in the world's virtue and terror, than I would from the anonymity of childlessness have thought possible.

I have tried to explore some of these issues in this book, with the aim of answering the larger question of what it is to turn from a woman into a mother. My definitions, of woman and of mother, remain vague, but the process continues to exert on me a real fascination. It is, I don't doubt, much the same process that it has always been, but the journey involved is, in my view, far longer for us than it was for our own mothers. Childbirth and motherhood are the anvil upon which sexual inequality was forged, and the women in our society whose responsibilities, expectations and experience are like those of men are right to approach it with trepidation. Women have changed, but their biological condition remains unaltered. As such motherhood provides a unique window to the history of our sex, but its glass is easily broken. I continue to marvel at the fact that every single member of our species has been born and brought to independence by so arduous a route. It is this work, requisitioned from a woman's life, that I have attempted to describe.

This book is a modest approach to the theme of motherhood, written in the first heat of its subject. It describes a period in which time seemed to go round in circles rather than in any chronological order, and so which I have tried to capture in themes rather than by the forgotten procession of its days. There will doubtless be other years for whose insights I will wish I had waited. Instead I have borrowed the insights of others by including in this book some discussion of those novels that I read or recalled during its writing, which seemed to me to give voice to my theme. It is a partial and personal selection: literature has long since discovered and documented this place of which I thought myself to be the first inhabitant, and there are countless poems and novels that could take the place of those I have chosen. It is more to illustrate the particular transformation of sensibility that motherhood effects than to find its most perfect expression that I have mentioned books at all: my experience of reading, indeed of culture, was profoundly changed by having a child, in the sense that I found the concept of art and expression far

more involving and necessary, far more human in its drive
to bring forth and create, than I once did.

For now, this is a letter, addressed to those women who
care to read it, in the hope that they find some companion-
ship in my experiences.

Forty Weeks

In the changing rooms at the swimming pool you can see the bodies of women. Naked, they have a narrative quality, like cave paintings; a quality muted by clothes and context, a quality seen only here, in this damp, municipal place where we are grouped anonymously, by gender. Though I too have the body of a woman, the sight still briefly arouses in me a child's fear, a mixture of revulsion and awe for these breasts and bellies and hips, this unidealised, primitive flesh which, forgetful here of its allure, seems composed purely of reproductive purpose. The hairdryers sing, the locker doors bang open and shut, the tiled floor of the shower room runs with unguents and foam. Veined, muscled legs stalk to and fro; bare arms untangle matted hair and towel skin that quivers with exertion. Breasts and bellies and hips, customised with moles and scars, with skin smocked or smooth, engraved like runes or blank as new-sculpted marble: declarative and material, they exist as objects, communicating by form alone. Sometimes there are children in the changing rooms and I see them stare in the way I used to stare, and half want to still: in illicit wonder and terror at the suggestiveness of the adult physiognomy, its frank protrusions and fur and patina of age or experience bespeaking untold mysteries of pleasure and pain, of copulation, gestation and birth. Like a trailer for a horror film, the adult body hints broadly at what must remain uneasily within the precincts of the imagination until legitimate entrance to its full unfolding is attained.

As a child, from the moment I gained some under-standing of what it entailed, I worried about childbirth. My understanding came without footnotes, without clauses stating that you didn't have to have a baby, let alone might not be able to: like all facts of life, it took a non-negotiable form. All I knew, looking at my narrow, recessless body, was that one day another body would come out of it, although it was not clear how or from where. As I understood it I was not to be fitted with some kind of extraction device at a later date. This same body held the promise of a future violence, like a Mexican pinata doll full of sweets. Some people kept those dolls, unable to inflict upon them the tragedy that was their calling, even at the spur of the most urgent, intran-sigent desire. Most people didn't. At children's parties in California, where I grew up, we used to beat them with a stick until they exploded and gave up their glorious contents. No exceptional understanding of the matter was required to work out that childbirth would be extremely painful. My early experiences of pain were quickly pressed into the service of this understanding. It seemed to me that an ability to tolerate physical discomfort was a necessary adjunct to the fact of my sex, and whenever I cut or bruised myself, or fell over or visited the dentist, I would feel not only pain but terror that I had felt it, that I had registered an injury so small when the fact of this great and mysterious agony lay so immovably in my future.

At school we were shown a film of a woman giving birth. She was naked, with thin, powerful arms and legs that waved out from the vast, afflicted hump of her belly, and her hair was long and tangled. She was not tucked up in bed, ringed with a bright halo of white-coated doctors and nurses. In fact, she didn't appear to be in hospital at all. She stood alone in a small room that was empty but for a low stool placed in the centre. I was disturbed by the sight of this stool. It seemed an inadequate defence against the onslaught that was to come. The camera gave out a dim, nocturnal picture, and the viewer's impression was of watching voyeuristically through a hole in the wall something terrible and secret, something doomed to travel beyond our comprehension and desire to look. The woman paced the room groaning and bellowing, like a lunatic or an animal in a cage. Occasionally she would lean against the wall for some minutes, her head in her hands, before flinging herself away with a cry to the opposite wall. It was as if she were fighting some invisible opponent: her solitude, amidst the noise and force of her responses, seemed strange. Presently I noticed that she was not, in fact, alone; another woman, this one fully clothed, was sitting quietly in a corner. Occasionally she murmured almost inaudibly, sounds which, though unhelpfully faint, were certainly encouraging. Her presence lent a degree of authority to the proceedings, but her failure to help or at least sympathise seemed inexplicably cruel. The naked woman tore at her matted hair and roared. Suddenly she staggered to the centre of the room and placed herself on the stool, one leg bent and the other flung dashingly to the side, hands clasped to her chest as if she were about to sing. Her companion rose and knelt before her. The camera, being stationary, did not offer us a close-up of this turn of events. In fact, the picture seemed to grow premonitorily darker and less distinct. The two women held their penumbral tableaux of communion for a moment; and then suddenly the clothed woman leaned forward, hands extended, and into them fell the small, thrashing body of a baby. The naked woman's final yell of pain fluted upwards into a yodel of delight.

'Natasha had married in the early spring of 1813,' writes Tolstoy of his romantic young heroine at the end of *War and Peace*, 'and in 1820 already had three daughters, besides a son for whom she had longed and whom she was now nursing. She had grown stouter and broader, so that it was difficult to recognise the slim, lively Natasha of former days in this robust motherly woman. Her features were more defined and had a calm, soft and serene expression. In her face there was none of the ever-glowing animation that had formerly burned there and constituted its charm. Now her face and body were often all that one saw, and her soul was not visible at all. All that struck the eye was a strong, handsome and fertile woman.'

In pregnancy, the life of the body and the life of the mind abandon the effort of distinctness and become fatally and historically intertwined. As a sequel to youth, beauty or independence, motherhood promises from its first page to be a longer and more difficult volume: the story of how Tolstoy's Natasha turned from trilling, beribboned heartbreaker into inscrutable matriarch, of how daughters become parents and heroines implacable opponents of the romantic plot. Tolstoy did not write this volume. Instead he wrote *Anna Karenina,* excavating the woman extant in the mother and demonstrating her power to destroy, for motherhood is a career in conformity from which no amount of subterfuge can liberate the soul without violence; and pregnancy is its boot-camp.

My arrival in this camp is meditated but not informed. I know about pregnancy only what everybody knows about it, which is what it looks like from the outside. I have walked past it many times. I have wondered what goes on behind its high walls. Knowing the pain which every inmate must endure as the condition of their release, I have imagined it to be a place in which some secret and specialised process of preparation occurs, in which confidential information is handed out in sealed envelopes that will explain this pain, that will render it painless. I tell my doctor that I am pregnant and he does a sum on a bit of paper involving dates. It is now July. He gives me a date in March of the following year. It takes me some time to realise that this is the day on which he expects my child to be born. He tells me to see the midwife. Close the door on your way out, he says.

The midwife gives me information, but of a particular sort: it concerns the things I can expect to happen to me, but not what she or anybody else intends to do about them. She tells me to come back in a couple of months. I had expected there to be at least some occupational aspect to pregnancy designed to mitigate fear. What am I going to do for all this time? Seeing my stricken face, she recommends one or two books I might read on the subject. I go and buy them and return home. Pregnancy lasts for two hundred and sixty-six days, forty weeks, nine months, or three trimesters, depending on how you choose to count it. The medical profession counts in weeks. The general public, for whom other people's pregnancies pass like life, count in months. I don't know who counts in trimesters, teachers perhaps, or women on their fifth baby. Only those who suffer, people wrongfully imprisoned, people with broken hearts, count days. I veer fretfully from one method to another, but the story of pregnancy is best recounted in trimesters. The first trimester is characterised by nausea and fatigue. The second trimester is characterised by a large stomach and a feeling of well-being. In the third trimester you may experience bloating around the face, swelling of wrists and ankles, varicose veins, piles, chronic heartburn, constipation, clumsiness, forgetfulness, fatigue, feelings of apprehension about the birth and a longing for pregnancy to be over.

Nowhere in these books, I notice, does it mention as a feature of pregnancy the dawning of some sort of under-standing of how the baby is supposed to come out. Illustrations of this event are amply supplied: they generally take the form of a series of cross-sections, the first showing the baby in the woman's stomach, the last showing the baby having come out of the woman's stomach. I begin to suspect that the experience is akin to that of being selected from amongst the passengers of an airborne jumbo jet to fly and then land the plane yourself. Occasionally there are photographs, images of women transfixed as if at the moment of death: grimacing, sweating, imploring, eyes screwed shut or turned heavenwards, their bodies drowning in a tangle of sheets and hospital wires or raised up by pain into cruciform postures, arms outstretched. It is as if some secret female history is unfolding in these photographs, a tale of suffering conspiratorially concealed. But even the frankness of its images does not seem to penetrate the mystery of childbirth. *Many women find labour easier when they adopt a vertical position,* reads the caption; or *The baby emerges in an atmosphere of timelessness and peace.*

My mother has always been fairly honest about her own experiences of birth. When the time comes, she says, take any drugs they offer you. I have had troubling hints from other women, too, women who bark with jaded laughter at the mention of the word 'pain', or who remark mysteriously that afterwards *you're never the same again.* Such clues are never explained; indeed, everything suddenly seems to go rather quiet, as if some vow of silence has been unintentionally broken. I myself decide to broadcast my experiences at every opportunity, once I've had them; but the fact that I have never personally encountered such a disciple of truth, have neither heard nor read during the course of my life a straightforward account of this most ubiquitous of happenings, suggests to me the presence of an additional horror surrounding the mystery: that somehow, during those tortured hours, some fundamental component of oneself is removed, so that afterwards although one looks and sounds more or less exactly as one did before, one is in fact a simulacrum, a brainwashed being programmed not to bear witness to the truth. I recall in the film *Invasion of the Body Snatchers* a moment of similar realisation, when one of only two remaining characters who have not been taken over by aliens reveals that he has, in fact, been taken over by aliens. The film ends with a close-up of the terror-striken face of his girlfriend, as she realises that she is alone now in a world of automatons.

The modern, privileged woman is a creature for whom the fact of her sex can remain, indefinitely if she chooses, a superficial characteristic. What do I understand by the term 'female'? A false thing; a repository of the cosmetic, a world of scented boutiques and tissue-wrapped purchases, of fake eyelashes, French unguents, powder and paint, a world in which words such as suffering, self-control and endurance occur, but usually in reference to weight loss; a world steeped in its own mild, voluntary oppression, a world at whose fringes one may find intersections to the real: to particular kinds of unhappiness, or discrimination, or fear, or to a whole realm of existence both past and present that grows more individuated and indeterminate and inarticulable as time goes by. What it once meant to be a woman, if such a meaning can ever be fixed, it no longer means; and yet in one, great sense, the sense of procreation, it means it still. The biological destiny of women remains standing amidst the ruins of their inequality, and in approaching it I have the sense of stepping off the proper path of my life, of travelling forwards but at some unbreachable distance; as if I had boarded a train and could see through the window the road on which I had always been, a road with which for a while my train ran parallel before gaining speed and moving steadily away to east or west, to a vista of unfamiliar hills, leaving everything vanishing behind it.

I go on a walking holiday in the Pyrenees. The only evidence, as yet, of my altered state is the fact that I am followed for the entire week by a swarm of small insects who mill about me like fans, like bodyguards. Towards the end of the week I leave the path to visit a frozen lake at high altitude. I cannot reconnect with my route without going all the way back down the mountain, and I decide to walk through the snow in the right direction in the hope of rejoining it on the other side of the pass. I set off around the lake, a preternatural arctic swirl from which the earth rises steeply like the sides of a bowl. These sides, being covered in snow and ice, are extremely slippery, and after I have crawled some way around the lake it becomes clear that I am in danger of sliding down beneath the ice and sinking to the bottom with the weight of my rucksack. I inch my way back and try going round the other side, where a faint path threads its way jaggedly and near-vertically upwards to the pass. At the top, in the tiny gap of the pass, I find a shrine containing a statue of the Virgin Mary. Superstitiously, I pray. In front of me there lies what appears to be the whole of France, miles below. The mountain sheers steeply downwards at my feet in a narrow snowy gully through which it appears I must descend. The snow looks fluffy and deep, like a cloud, the gully bottom as far away as the earth seen from the sky. A sort of madness seizes me. Like a child who believes she can fly, my sense of the reality of my own body and its limitations disappears. The beautiful and terrible vista seems suddenly tiny and magical, like the world of a doll through which I am convinced I can take giant steps. For days I have inched and trudged and clung to these mountains and now, delightedly, as if I had reached heaven, I jump down into the snow with a shriek of abandon. The snow, of course, is not snow. It is ice. I understand what I have done too late as the sky and mountain fly past me in a blur of speed. The slope is very steep and I plummet down it quickly on my back, frantically trying to dig my feet and elbows into the rough, glass-hard surface, but my rucksack acts as a sort of sledge, making me go faster. In front of me, like a long ski-run, the mountain dips away and then levels out far below before meeting a wall of rock. My skin burns as it speeds over the ice. Like a stone I begin to skip and bounce, cartwheeling in the air. I am, I realise, utterly unprepared to meet pain, even though I know that very soon I will probably break my neck. There is, as far as I can see, nothing that will stop me from falling and falling, and though I try to summon something from myself, some understanding, some ability to prepare, some native acknowledgement or recognition from my body of the prospect of its own demise, I remain the same as I always have been; in a stupor, certainly, of terror and disbelief, but myself all the same. It is this unexpected fact that frightens me more than anything else. I hit a large boulder, and as my body hurtles up and over it I catch frantically at it with my fingernails. They tear off like paper but I cling to the rock with my hands and arms, clasping it in a mortal embrace. Abruptly, I stop. Around the boulder there is a pool of shingle on to which I presently edge myself. My arms are numb and running with blood. My tiny rocky island is about halfway down the slope. I sit on it and cry as evening begins to tint the vast, enamel-bright mountain. I appear to have dispersed any claim I might ever have made to courage or sense or humanity. I have surrendered the pretence of personality, its fraudulent offers of shelter, its nonexistent provision. I can help nobody, can protect nobody, can only sit and cry over the sorry fact of myself, a fact I appear only to have learned in the shadow of its destruction.

The question of how I am to get down the rest of the gulley before night falls remains unanswered. Presently an apparition, at first ant-like then slowly larger, approaches from far beneath me. A man is ice-picking his way up the gulley using ropes and crampons. He has not, like a mother, come to gather me up and take me home. Like a different kind of mother, he intends to instruct me in how properly to descend an ice field on my own. You always face the mountain, he says. You make holes for your own feet and hands. Filled with self-pity, I am angered that he does not intend to take me down himself. I had imagined a stretcher, helicopters perhaps. I am injured and afraid of the slope, and unsure, more importantly, of whether I have the nerve to move at all. I hope that he will notice this, but we are not in an emotional place. I am merely emotional. Having given me my instructions, the man turns and proceeds upwards through the gloaming. I remove my rucksack and throw it down the mountain to make things easier. It bounces and flies down and disappears like a pebble. I know that I have no choice but to go back out on to the ice, and consequently I go, and climb slowly down, with the reality of falling, the breathing memory of it at my back. What I feel, it seems, is no obstacle to what I am able to do. Having lived always in a world of feeling, I have not yet in my life experienced so direct a contest between the two. Sometimes, while I am climbing down, I think that I would prefer to be like this, to be practical and brave. But that night in the tent, I am privately distraught with fear of what happened. I wonder whether there exists some superior response to what has occurred. I wonder whether my survival matters more or less than my terror. I have not yet thought much about motherhood, but I suspect that it combines fact and feeling in exactly this disturbing way.

Back home I get into bed and stay there for two weeks. I appear to be suffering from vertigo. The force of gravity, the dizzy revolutions of the earth, my fear of the vertical, keep me pinned to my back. My insides stir premonitorily with nausea. Beneath the covers my body grows warm and soft: my calloused feet, my flesh toughened by exposure and climbing, seem to yield and melt and dilate as the days go by. When I get out of bed again I have become a cocoon.

*

Just wiggle your hips up and down, commands the sonographer, and we'll see if we can get it to move. On the computer screen beside the bed, a small, monochrome crustacean lies in a snowstorm of static. Obediently, resentfully, I shake my hips. Come on, the sonographer urges the creature harshly, let's see you move! She presses the scanner down harder on my stomach. The creature waves its thin arms as if distressed. I feel that I should be protecting it from torments of this sort but say nothing. I am told to shake my hips for some further minutes, wondering whether this is a medical procedure, but the sight of the creature moving is apparently for nothing but my own entertainment. I am reminded of a western in which an Indian is made to dance by a cowboy firing bullets at his feet. I am asked if I would like a photograph, and receive a slip of shiny paper on which the screen's snowy image is imprinted.

I look at it on the way home. The creature is seen indistinctly from the side, reclining in shadows, its head a brainy bubble attached to the pale keyboard of its spine. I have also been presented with a spray of leaflets by the hospital, about diet, acupuncture, yoga, antenatal classes, parentcraft classes, hypnotism and waterbirth, none of which contains any information I don't already know, for modern pregnancy is governed by a regime breathtaking in the homogeneity of its propaganda, its insignia, its language. No Korean cheerleading team was ever ruled with so iron a rod as pregnant women in the English-speaking world. I long to receive some signal of subterfuge, some coded reference to a resistance. My sex has become an exiguous, long-laid, lovingly furnished trap into which I have inadvertently wandered and from which now there is no escape. I have been tagged, as if electronically, by pregnancy. My womanly movements are being closely monitored.

The rules and regulations of pregnancy are artfully laid out in a volume entitled *Emma's Diary*. Have you got a copy of *Emma?* I am asked at the hospital, in what is patently not a reference to Jane Austen. Take another, just in case. Emma, I learn, is a fictional character created by the National Health Service who has written a week-by-week diary account of her pregnancy. She has a husband called Peter and a fondness for exclamation marks. She has neat brown hair and blue eyes and wears well-ironed clothes in pastel shades. She has two friends, both of whom are also pregnant. The first is an unmarried good-time girl with a wavering boyfriend. The second is an older black woman with an unreconstructed husband and two daughters. Emma's friendship with these two ladies, which Peter gallantly allows her to pursue, takes the form of her recording of the difficulties they encounter in lives that are rather more complicated, we are given to understand, than Emma's own. Emma reports that her unmarried friend is arguing a lot with her boyfriend. I'm so glad Peter and I don't do that! Her other friend's husband, meanwhile, is copping off the childcare. I'm really glad, says Emma, that Peter and I have agreed to share everything equally! Emma informs us that she has cut her lustrous hair short 'for convenience'. Peter, in tight pleated trousers, is pictured hoovering around the sofa on which she lies leafing through a magazine. He does that on Saturday mornings, to give her a break. Together they decorate the nursery and buy baby clothes. Emma's parents come to stay for the weekend and do DIY around the house. Her father tells her she is 'blooming'. Emma is fastidious on points of health and safety. Unpasteurised cheese and alcohol do not pass her lips. Even one cigarette a day, she reflects, would be harmful for the baby, and we are amazed the thought has even crossed her mind. She supports and promotes the existence of baby-exploiting multinational companies and their environmentally unfriendly products, of which each pregnant woman is promised an introductory pack courtesy of Emma on arrival of their baby. She is, confusingly, passionate on the subject of breastfeeding. She hopes to endure labour without the aid of drugs, and expects the baby to be a boy. I turn to the end immediately. The baby is a girl. She calls it Jane. She did manage to get through labour without drugs. It was bad, she says, but not as bad as I expected. This expectation has been well concealed by Emma from her diary. What form, I wish to know, did it take? I myself have no happier or more rational expectation of labour than I have of being murdered. And yet the suggestion must surely be that labour is not so bad after all, for I cannot believe that Emma possesses a particularly lively imagination. I think of the women I know who have had children, none of whom has remarked of birth that it wasn't nearly as bad as they were expecting. Most appear unable to speak about the subject at all, except one, who told me that at one point she begged the midwife to shoot her.

Preparation, I am repeatedly told in my leaflets, is the pregnant woman's defence against pain. People who are tense and out of touch with their bodies, people who resist labour, above all people who are afraid of pain feel more pain. If this sort of statement is a threat, its objective appears to be the encouragement of a curious communality. Joining groups, attending classes and courses, enlisting the help of your partner or a friend in the business of preparation are all recommended means of curing yourself of the faults of hubris, terror and independence of mind before labour commences. The literature tactfully tones down references to the ultimately solitary nature of childbirth, and to the fact that attending classes for it is like attending classes for death: indeed, every effort is made to strip the process of any personal significance at all, so that having read a certain number of these leaflets I am no longer sure whether it is I who will be going through labour or the woman in the orange tracksuit demonstrating with a grapefruit. Although it is not stated as such, as I understand it, by making yourself into a different person – one who breathes deeply, one who does exercises, one whose partner is willing to massage you with oil at all times of day and night – you give yourself a chance if not of lessening the rigours of pregnancy and the pain of childbirth, then at least of believing that it is happening to someone else.

Books about pregnancy go into this process of transformation, or sublimation, in sinister detail. You are offered a list of foods to eat, recipes for how to combine them, and occasionally photographs of the finished result, with captions such as *Salad* or *Bowl of Granola*. You are told, with the help of illustrations, how to get into bed, how to lie in it, and how to get up again. You are told, again with illustrations, how to make love. Possible conversations you might have with your partner concerning the impending birth and parenthood are detailed. You can conduct these over a cocktail if you like; non-alcoholic for you, of course! Find recipes for non-alcoholic cocktails on page 73. A section on antenatal appointments advises you to take a book or magazine, or perhaps some knitting, in case you have to wait. When you go to have your ultrasound scan, leave plenty of time to find the correct hospital department. When you have found it and your name has been called, go into the scanning room. Remove your clothes and lie on the couch while the operator performs the scan. Go shopping for baby clothes before you get too large. Decorate the nursery, preferably in primary colours using lead-free paint. At night, when you can't sleep and your mind is racing, violently suppress this insurrection of identity and use the time to get in touch with your baby. Afflicted by sleeplessness, I follow this last piece of advice, but my communications with the baby always end up taking the undignified form of my pleading with it not to hurt me. As my stomach grows bigger I realise that getting in touch with it is about as useful as a field getting in touch with the motorway being built through it.

Like a bad parent, the literature of pregnancy bristles with threats and the promise of reprisal, with ghoulish hints at the consequences of thoughtless actions. Eat pâté and your baby will get liver damage. Eat blue cheese and your baby will get listeria, a silent and symptomless disease that will nonetheless leave your baby hideously deformed. Stroke the cat and your baby will get toxoplasmosis, a silent and symptomless disease that will nonetheless leave your baby hideously deformed. A temperature of more than 104 degrees sustained for several days could damage your baby in the first seven weeks of gestation, so don't use saunas, have hot baths, or for that matter wear a jersey at any point in pregnancy lest your baby be hideously deformed. Don't drink or smoke, you murderer. Don't take aspirin. Wear a seatbelt when you travel in a car; you can loosen the lower strap if you have problems stretching it over your abdomen. Anyone thinking that pregnancy is the one time in their life when they are allowed to be fat can think again. Don't eat cakes, biscuits, refined white flour, chocolate, sweets, fizzy drinks or chips. *When you raise your fork to your lips*, reads one book on this subject, *look at it and think, Is this the best bite I can give my baby? If the answer is no, put your fork down.*

The baby plays a curious role in the culture of pregnancy. It is at once victim and autocrat. It is a being destined to live only in the moment of perfection that is its birth, after which it degenerates and decays, becomes human and sinful, cries and is returned to the realm of the real. But in pregnancy the baby is a wonder, a miracle, an expiation. The literature dwells upon its formation week by week, the accretion of its tiny fingers and toes, its perfect little nails, its large, lidless, innocent eyes. Commerce with this being is actively sought. Most books claim you can feel its movements in the fourteenth week of pregnancy, little flutters, like the wings of butterflies. (A rather more robust, and hence outdated, volume informs me that this is just wind: proper movements are unlikely to be felt until a month later. Don't worry about falling over, the book cheerfully adds, or indeed about car accidents or falling down the stairs. The only thing capable of harming the baby is a really forceful blow with a heavy object directly to the abdomen.) In the seventeenth week the baby develops hearing. It can hear your voice, the voice of its mother! It has plenty of time, I feel, to get over and indeed tire of this development.

When the baby is being active, I am instructed to smooth my hands over my belly and speak or sing to it. It will quieten. You have soothed your baby.

Such *faux* motherhood, solitary, perfect and bizarre, is not, I notice, recommended for women who have already had a child, and not only because they are less gullible. In one book, I find a section dedicated to these unfortunates, entitled 'Pregnant Again'. It is very short. It mentions the reactions you can expect from other people on informing them of your second or subsequent pregnancy. What, *again?* they may say; or, Haven't you had enough? You will be feeling, the section adds, physically and emotionally drained. Your body, used up by a previous pregnancy, will sag and bloat. What with all the incessant tidying up, washing and cooking created by children who fling carefully prepared dishes to the floor and empty out boxes of toys as quickly as you can fill them, as well as waking up several times a night and screaming, you probably won't have any time to yourself to think about this pregnancy. You may feel that you cannot possibly find the extra love to give to a new baby. You may be existing on burgers and fries. You may worry about your relationship with your partner, about money, about whether you need a bigger house. At least labour won't be so bad this time, it adds, because all your muscles will have been bent out of shape by the last one.

I telephone the hospital to book an antenatal class.

You're too late, I'm told, we're full. You should have booked earlier. I wasn't pregnant earlier, I reply. I see that I have entered a world of obsessive foresight, in which women at my stage of pregnancy are now putting their unborn children down for desirable schools. A feeling of panic at being left behind, unprepared and hence exposed to pain like someone abandoned unarmed in a jungle full of wild animals, seizes me. I make several more telephone calls and finally find a pregnancy yoga class being conducted in a suburban community centre. I turn up and sit with six or seven other pregnant women in a circle on the floor. The teacher sits in our midst, cross-legged. I have not yet experienced such a gathering of my own species. We appear imprisoned behind our stomachs like people behind bars, like people who need help. I feel a certain relief at our communality, a sense of assuagement. I wonder why I have ridiculed and resisted it. The teacher tells us of her own experiences of birth. They are yogic and positive. She tells us of her moment of illumination, when she realised that pregnant women just needed people to be nice to them, and that given the short supply of such people, the solution was for pregnant women to be nice to *each other*. So here we are, we are told, about to be nice to each other! The teacher flings her arms in the air and laughs effervescently. We are instructed to breathe deeply. We adopt various positions. Birth is mentioned several times, vaguely. We stand against a wall and do things with our legs. One girl can do the splits. Presently we are told to find partners. The instruction cauterises my enthusiasm. I don't want a partner. In fact, I want to go home as quickly as possible. Nevertheless I select, or am selected, mutely. We are, it appears, going to give each other a massage. This is what is known as being nice. We are told to divide ourselves into masseur and massee. I am massee. My partner, a girl with fuzzy white hair, a deep tan and a nose ring, whose name I have forgotten, proceeds with her work. I close my eyes. I am as rigid as steel. The teacher issues her instructions in a soft voice, as if someone were asleep next door. I leave my body and drift determinedly elsewhere, while tension rises in me like a tide. After a very long time, the massage stops. I meet the girl's eye awkwardly and laugh. My own tenure as masseur I embark on with professional zeal. I am not going to be found wanting. The girl's skin is foreign and private, and though I will gentleness upon myself I am brisk with the consciousness of invasion. Afterwards cookies and tea are produced. I make an excuse and leave. Glancing back from the door I see the women all sitting in a circle with their mugs, their silhouettes fertile and vulnerable. No one is saying much. I feel like a man, caught in some shameful act of abandonment.

Winter draws in. I begin to feel a more or less constant despair at my predicament. In the mornings, when I wake up, I observe the rising mountain of my stomach and have to fight surges of intense claustrophobia. With many weeks of pregnancy remaining I am marooned as far from myself as I will ever be. It is not just abstinence, stripped of the pleasure of the possibility of giving in to temptation, that grates upon me; nor even the extremity of my physical transformation, nor the strange pains that accompany it, nor the surreally floundering being that writhes like a live fish in my stomach, nor the disempowerment I feel, the vulnerability to others' eyes and assumptions. (Don't worry, says a young man with no arms, bitterly, walking past me at the bus stop, it won't be like me. I want to run after him and reclaim as my rightful property whatever glance he thought it was I had given him. I don't care if it is like you, I want to say, I'm not like that, I just want to get out of this.) It is the population of my privacy, as if the door to my room were wide open and strangers were in there, rifling about, that I find hard to endure. It is as if I have been arrested or called to account, summoned by the tax inspector, isolated and searched. I am living not freely but in some curious tithe. I have surrendered my solitude and become, for these nine months, a bridge, a link, a vehicle. I read newspaper reports of women in America being prosecuted for harming their unborn foetuses and wonder how this can be; how the body can become a public space, like a telephone box, that can unlawfully vandalise itself. It is my fear of authority, of conformity, that is pricked by such stories. I am someone who has always dreaded the discovery and announcement of my shortcomings. Now it is as if some spy is embedded within me, before whose scrutiny I am guilty and self-conscious. It is not, I feel sure, the baby who exerts this watchful pressure: it is the baby's meaning for other people, the world's sense of ownership stating its claim.

But I am not merely the chauffeur of this precious cargo; I am also its box, its container, and while my fastnesses are regulated and supervised, the manner in which I will be broken open on arrival at our destination remains shrouded in mystery. *Some women find birth the most intensely pleasurable experience of their lives,* I read. This miraculous claim is made by proponents of natural, or 'active', birth. It is an attractive one; the best the medical establishment can offer, by contrast, is that it won't hurt too much if you submit to being forcefully injected with powerful drugs. Having been brought up to think it remarkable that after centuries of agony and death in childbirth women had finally been offered anaesthetics, it takes me some time to come around to the notion of natural birth. It is a philosophy based largely on the birth experiences of women in primitive societies. Who and where these women are is not gone into in any detail: the important thing about them is that when their time comes, they do not dial 911 and proffer their flank for a syringe. They go through it naturally, because that is what they have always done, because the medical establishment has not meddled with their natural instincts, because their traditions of birth remain intact: and the thing is, *it doesn't hurt.* Pain, in other words, has been created by its expectation, and also by the fact that MEN make women lie on their backs and stay still during labour, when any primitive woman could tell you to stick with your sisters, stay on your feet, and keep MEN well out of it. Diagrams are supplied, the same diagrams that illustrate the baby coming out of the woman's stomach except turned the other way to demonstrate the force of gravity. I wonder whether it is permitted to stay on your feet, but in hospital. It's up to you, comes the answer; as long as you realise that hospital is a place where MEN are, and hence that as soon as you set foot in one your chances of artificial rupture of membranes, chemical induction of labour, electronic foetal monitoring, stalled labour, epidural, paralysis, forceps delivery, Caesarean section and the need for the baby to be artifically respirated afterwards are greatly increased. Why not have it at home, amongst friends, in peaceful surroundings? In a warm birthpool perhaps? Photographs of this procedure are supplied. The pool, a sort of deep inflatable ring surrounded by house plants, seems very crowded. In it are a naked woman with long plaits, a heavily bearded man in very small swimming trunks and several children.

A sense of political outrage at the patriarchal medicalisation of birth, unfortunately, is not a sufficient qualification for going it alone. Yogic preparation, in this arena, is more important than ever. Natural birth relies on the labouring woman following her instincts. I have certainly mislaid these instincts, if I ever had them. My instinct for avoiding hospital, however, is vigorously alive. I know, from lengthy childhood illness, that hospital is a place of steel, a place where things happen, where event is irresistible. Secretly, I imagine that if I never go to hospital I won't have to have the baby at all. I read more books about natural childbirth. With every exhortation to draw closer to my own physical state, I retreat further into a deluded solitude. My will, my power to evade pain, becomes entrancing, but not in the sense intended: I have found, at last, a narrative of childbirth that is as unreal as my own vision of it. Now that I am closer to labour, other women begin to drop louder hints about it. I hear of episiotomies, of Caesareans in which the anaesthetic didn't quite work, of badly sewn stitches, of painful internal examinations, of fifty-hour confinements. Words like mutilation and tearing are mentioned. I no longer know whether I am more afraid of the pain of childbirth or the interventions it invites. I tell the hospital that I have decided to have the baby at home. The midwife brings a sinister case of implements to the house, and I am close to physically attacking her. I catch a glimpse of scalpels, scissors, needles. Why do we need those? I want to know, somewhat hysterically. She insists on leaving the case in my bedroom, so that if I go into labour early it will all be to hand. I sense that the moment I have always feared is drawing closer, closing in: the moment not of birth, nor even of pain, but of recognition, of the arrival of some terrible apparition whose shadow I have fancied myself to have glimpsed so often in my life. At night I open my eyes and look at the midwife's case in the dark. In its dense, concentrated blackness, like a bomb, I see a long moment of forestalled horror, of disbelief, of dammed-up but pressingly, explosively imminent reality.

Then, suddenly, things change. It is February and the days are brief and pale, the nights deep and dark as lakes. The year is creaking on its hinges: soon it will open and let in the light of spring. I have been waiting for this light as for the signal of my readiness, but it never comes. A month of pregnancy remains, and I begin to bleed. I report it to the midwife and against my protests she takes me to the hospital. Once there I am taken to the ultrasound room. A crowd gathers around my prone body. The snowy images appear once more on the screen. The sonographer leans forward, clicks at her keyboard, scrutinises. It's unbelievable, she announces baldly. The consultant also leans forward. They probe the screen with disbelieving fingers. It's all the wrong way round, says the sonographer. The placenta is completely blocking the cervix. The baby can't come out. See? She addresses this to me. Attentively, obediently, I look, and see something black and swirling that resembles outer space. A murmur of outrage goes up. This should have been spotted earlier. It is a life-threatening condition. Had I gone ahead with my plans to have the baby at home, I am told, we would both have died. I look at the screen while they discuss it. The scanner has wandered slightly in the sonographer's distracted hand, and suddenly, out of the darkness, the sleeping face of my daughter emerges. It fills the screen, pale and tranquil as a moon, ethereal as a ghost. It is the face of a person, not putative but real, hovering, coming in, waiting to exist. No one else notices it. The sonographer gestures in the air with the scanner and it is gone.

I am told I must now remain in hospital. Rebelliously, desperately, I discharge myself and go home. The next day I come back and surrender. It is a Sunday evening. The hospital is dark and deserted, as if its customers observed office hours. A militant junior doctor keen to practise inserting things into veins falls upon me hungrily. She offers blood tests, the implantation of a canula. I refuse them. Quietly enraged, she disappears and returns with back-up. It is explained to me that I must undergo these procedures. I argue and eventually submit to the blood tests alone. The junior doctor stabs the needle into my arm as if she were playing championship darts. Then she stabs it into the other arm. Blood seeps under the skin to form two large red patches, like birthmarks, up my arms. Chastened, I am put to bed in a ward. I spend the next three days there, and am visited by gangs of junior doctors who have heard about the canula incident and want to exact revenge. I fight them off. Eventually a tall, kind girl comes to my bed late one night. Let's just put it in, shall we? she says. I concede my hand, and she pushes the valve into a vein on the back of it and goes away. The consultant comes to see me. He has a jolly, Tyrolean look about him. If you'd been born a hundred and fifty years ago, he says, you'd be dead by now. I reply that most people would and he laughs uncomprehendingly. I am to have a Caesarean section. Which day would you like it? he asks with a smile. I opt for Wednesday. I ask whether the baby is ready to be removed and am assured that it is. He has delivered babies like kittens, like feathers, like thoughts, babies that hardly exist. I sense he would like them not to be in there in the first place, but to grow them himself in a seed tray. Mine has had eight months, apparently a decadent quantity of time for this hospital.

The other women in the ward are having Caesareans too. There is no groaning or tearing of hair. Each morning, one or two of them leave the ward on foot and are wheeled back an hour or so later carrying babies. They are taken to other rooms. Now that I have been given a day, an hour and a demarcated sphere of anxiety, I grow mute and limp with acceptance. I recognise this clinical, timetabled world as my destined place. I laugh at my flirtation with natural birth as if at a strange dream or delusion. The anaesthetist comes to visit. General or local? General, I say immediately. He persuades me to accept double local. People are rude about you in theatre when you're under general, he says. You'll be glad afterwards, he adds as he leaves. For three days I eat nothing, read nothing, think nothing. Outside the weather is pellucid, beautiful. Through the windows the world seems stalled and peaceful. I feel as if I am at the end of my life, drifting in a hushed, airy limbo. When Wednesday comes, I make panicked telephone calls at dawn in a spasm of terror. I return to bed and a nurse comes. She is not on a round: she has come for me. Birth has me within its sights. She ministers to my body, preparing it as if for burial. How are you today? she says as she works. Then she leaves me alone. Presently a midwife comes. They're ready for you, she says. We get in a lift and descend two floors. We weave our way along corridors, turning left and right. Then we push through double doors and enter the operating theatre, a room that reminds me uncannily of pictures I have seen of execution chambers. In its centre, like an altar, is the operating table. The room is filled with people in masks. As soon as they see me they surge forward, taking my arms, pressing hands against my back, bearing me like a strong current towards the operating table. I am sat on it and immediately am assailed from all sides. Someone is injecting something into my hand. A group behind me are injecting something into my back. I look down to see a giant, three-pronged valve being pushed bloodily into a vein. I don't know to which front to send my defences, where to concentrate my powers of endurance, and so I give up and hang my head. Presently I realise that I am now lying on the table. The attendants are heaving my body from side to side. A cloth screen is erected over my chest. Somebody sprays a blast of something cold on to my skin. Can you feel that? he shouts. Yes, I shout back. And that? Yes! This seems a worryingly primitive procedure. I hope that he's heard me. A woman is holding my head, a hand over each of my ears. She removes one hand to tell me that they have made the incision. There is some tugging and pushing and wiggling, which I feel through a thick blanket of anaesthetic. Everyone is talking. A radio is playing and a man is singing along to the music. The woman goes away. I can see my own face reflected in the broad lamp above me. I look at the clock and see that only ten minutes have passed since I left the ward. What's happening? I say. My voice sounds preternatural coming out of my dead body. I fear suddenly that I have been forgotten, that I am going to be left dismantled, a talking head on a table. I fear that my soul is being uncaged and allowed to fly away. Nobody replies to my question. Some transfer of significance has occurred: I feel it, feel the air move, feel time begin to pour down a new tributary. The world adjusts itself. The doctors hold the baby up over the screen so that I can see her. She is livid and blue and her face is a rictus of shock and fear. I recognise her immediately from the scan. Only I knew the secret of her tranquillity, the floating world of her gestation. She is borne off to the far side of the room, away from me, and as if she were a light I fall deeper into shadow the further away she goes. The midwives crowd around her. I lose sight of her but her cries reach me like messages. Presently she emerges clothed and wrapped in a blanket. Her father takes her and holds her. His offers of friendship must suffice, must compensate for her lack of proper passage, for the clock of experience has started ticking and won't wait for me. Her life has begun.

Lily Bart's Baby

Edith Wharton's 1905 novel *The House of Mirth* asks the question of what a woman is if she is not a wife, a mother, a daughter. Wharton herself was none of these things. She married, a marriage of class and convenience, but lived separately, estranged, and finally on a different continent from her husband. Her parents were dead. She had no children. Her right to exist derived from her wealth, inherited and then earned by her writing. Latterly she had a large collection of lapdogs, to whom she was obsessively devoted, and she found philanthropy: living in France during the First World War, she set up refuges and schools for orphaned children.

Lily Bart, the heroine of *The House of Mirth,* is an orphan. The story of her life corresponds inversely to that of Wharton's, like the negative of a photograph. Lily's parents died leaving her penniless. She has neither education nor talents nor training. She is very beautiful; a beauty cultivated to fetch a price by a mother who died before she could oversee the sale. Lily has been abandoned to her vanity like the hothouse flower her name suggests left out in the cold and rain. The only thing she knows how to do is to exist, beautifully; to be an asset to a room, an arm, a buttonhole. She spends her time subsisting in the borrowed water of others' wealth, moving from country house to country house, always on the brink of outright penury and utterly vulnerable to falling out of fashion. Other women's husbands pursue her: she packs her bags and moves on to the next party. Wives and rivals turn jealous: she finds new friends, anyone with the hospitality to ensure her survival. She works harder than a skivvy at tact, flattery and charm, but trouble pursues her. Wealthy suitors somehow melt away from her grasp. Rumour sticks to her. Time waits on her, running its fingers over her pretty face. She meets a man called Lawrence Seldon, a poor, cultivated lawyer to whom she is strongly attracted, but their mutual prejudice divides them. She has been programmed to find material meaning for herself; he, in what is itself a form of vanity, to disdain vanity and greed; and yet he haunts her as she finally descends into poverty and social ignominy, haunts her with the suspicion that there was something else, that she stood at the door to a different realm of being and did not open it. On her way home one night to the squalid New York boarding house where she has finally fetched up, she meets a servant-girl to whom she once, in better days, showed charity. Shocked by Lily's haggard appearance, the girl invites her home to warm herself. In her firelit kitchen is a baby, which Lily is given to hold. Later that night, beset by exhaustion, illness and hunger, utterly alone, Lily accidentally takes an overdose of laudanum; and as she dies, the baby returns to her as a strange hallucination.

Such a vision of the solidarity of life had never before come to Lily. She had had a premonition of it in the blind motions of her mating-instinct; but they had been checked by the disintegrating influences of the life about her. All the men and women she knew were like atoms whirling away from each other in some wild centrifugal dance: her first glimpse of the continuity of life had come to her that evening in Nettie Struther's kitchen.

The poor little working-girl who had found strength to gather up the fragments of her life, and build herself a shelter with them, seemed to Lily to have reached the central truth of existence. It was a meagre enough life, on the grim edge of poverty, with scant margin for possibilities of sickness or mischance, but it had the frail audacious permanence of a bird's nest built on the edge of a cliff – a mere wisp of leaves and straw, yet so put together that the lives entrusted to it may hang safety over the abyss . . .

Tonight the drug seemed to work more slowly than usual: each passionate pulse had to be stilled in turn, and it was long before she felt them dropping into abeyance, like sentinels falling asleep at their posts. But gradually the sense of complete subjugation came over her . . . Tomorrow would not be so difficult after all: she felt sure that she would have the strength to meet it. She did not quite remember what it was that she had been afraid to meet, but the uncertainty no longer troubled her. She had been unhappy and now she was happy – she had felt herself alone, and now the sense of loneliness had vanished.

She stirred once, and turned on her side, and as she did so, she suddenly understood why she did not feel herself alone. It was odd – but Nettie Struther's child was lying on her arm: she felt the pressure of its little head against her shoulder. She did not know how it had come there, but she felt no great surprise at the fact, only a gentle penetrating thrill of warmth and pleasure. She settled herself into an easier position, hollowing her arm to pillow the round downy head, and holding her breath lest a sound should disturb the sleeping child.

As she lay there she said to herself that there was something she must tell Seldon, some word she had found that should make life clear between them. She tried to repeat the word, which lingered vague and luminous on the far edge of thought – she was afraid of not remembering it when she woke; and if she

48

could only remember it and say it to him, she felt that everything would be well.

Slowly the thought of the word faded, and sleep began to enfold her. She struggled faintly against it, feeling that she ought to keep awake on account of the baby; but even this feeling was gradually lost in an indistinct sense of drowsy peace, through which, of a sudden, a dark flush of loneliness and terror tore its way.

She started up again, cold and trembling with the shock: for a moment she seemed to have lost her hold of the child. But no – she was mistaken – the tender pressure of its body was still close to hers: the recovered warmth flowed through her once more, she yielded to it, sank into it, and slept.

The baby is the symbol not just of Lily's exclusion from the human life-cycle, nor of the vulnerability, the helplessness that marks her life and her life's end: it is also the vision of her squandered femininity, a ghostly image of mother and child, their bodies entwined, rising from the brittle, broken shell of her useless beauty. Through this image Lily finally finds the physical warmth, the closeness, the commitment that has been lacking in her relationships with men. There lay words, banter, bridled lust, gossip, calculation and adornment, all artifice-bright: here are love and responsibility, resolution, provision, peace, and the mercy of sleep and darkness that veils for a moment the prospect of death. It is not to the image of Lawrence Seldon that her frustrated body cleaves in its last hour: it is not sex – not commerce – but possession for which finally she yearns, possession of a living thing. Of all the many houses through which she has passed, the grand, cruel cattle-markets of men and women, exquisitely furnished with betrayal, boredom, greed and desire, it is only in this last, poor place that she finds something she can for a moment possess.

The baby and I are conveyed home through the streets of London in a taxi; like a cortège after a royal wedding driving through cheering crowds, a conventionally great moment underpinned by the suspicion of deep unfamiliarity, entertained in the glare of the utterly inescapable. We are, I have no doubt, a couple, a pair. I have not written off the many fleshly associations she has with others, but they have yet to make themselves real. All that is clear at this point is that I have replicated, like a Russian doll. I left home one; I have come back two.

It is only when I walk through the front door to my house that I realise things have changed. It is as if I have come to the house of someone who has just died, someone I loved, someone I can't believe has gone. The rooms, the furniture, the pictures and possessions all wear an unbearable patina of familiarity: standing there I feel bludgeoned by tragedy, as though I were standing in the irretrievable past. Minutes later the same rooms, the same possessions arouse in me a terrible panic, the panic of confinement. A violent anger seizes me at the sight of them; I recoil from their closeness as if in dislike. I feel burdened with secrets; an adulterous desire sets me apart from myself, fills me with both longing and revulsion for that which I have betrayed. I cannot explain these feelings. Instead I sit on the sofa and cry.

The baby is very small, I am repeatedly told. Her skin is brushed with blue. Her eyes remain closed. I, meanwhile, am disabled by my scar and can barely walk. We are still so close to our sundering that neither of us seems entire: the painful stump of our jointness, livid and fresh, remains. I don't quite understand what has happened and therefore I determine to conduct myself as though nothing had. I make tea and phone calls; I invite people round. They exclaim when I open the door, fully dressed, normal: at the returned fact of me, like an undelivered letter. Where's it gone? they laugh, pointing at my stomach. Pregnancy is a hallucination now. The mystery of the baby inside me has passed unsolved.

My ownership of my daughter is preoccupying, uncertain and fraught. In hospital I felt immediately a sort of animal-like habituation with her presence; at home I am in transactional shock, as if I had gone out and bought something extremely expensive, something for which in the shop I felt the fiercest, most private desire, and were now regarding it with shrivelled courage in my sitting room. I show it to other people, fearing their assessment. I let them touch and even hold it, silently frantic at the damage they might do, desperate to have it back. I both want and fear it, and yet can consummate neither my desire nor my fear, can neither use nor relinquish this precious purchase, for my feelings obstruct each other and hold me in a kind of dead-lock. My daughter sleeps on, pale and silent. She begins to seem to me not subject to crass analogies with shopping at all, but rather autonomous and self-possessed. I wonder whether she, in fact, knows what to do, and will inform us presently; whether her hours of rumination are being devoted to the formation of some kind of manifesto laying out exactly how we are to conduct things. She seems very *good*, I say helplessly to the midwife when she visits. The midwife laughs. They usually explode around the third day, she says. She illustrates this explosion with her hands.

One evening the baby opens her eyes. We take photographs of her, like something rare glimpsed in the wild. She stares at the cruel flash, unblinking. She stares at us. Her gaze is like a clear sky, unclouded by recognition, judgement, emotion. I feel frightened for her. We could be people who didn't care for her. We could, after all, be anybody. She closes her eyes. We put her in our bed between us. Later, during the night, I wake to find her staring at me again in the dark. She doesn't blink. Already her expression has changed, has acquired a layer of depth. I try to go back to sleep, but my sense that I am still pinioned by this disconcerting regard makes it impossible to keep my eyes closed. Guiltily, I find something eerie in it, as if the baby were absorbing information from me at high speed while I slept; as if she had been sent not to replace me exactly, but to use me as a sort of base or HQ where she would receive her instructions and await her readiness to head off on her top-secret mission. She cries briefly and I feed her. At intervals I change her nappy. Occasionally, hopefully, I remove a blanket or add one. She closes her eyes and opens them again. We wait, as if for her to state her purpose, or for her people to come from their planet and retrieve her.

In this brief period, while the baby lies enshrined in her separateness – or is receiving, as I now see it, the slow shock of that separateness, is being administered the powerful and momentarily paralysing charge of her humanity – I feel a profound bewilderment. It is as if I am unable to find any connection between my physical implication in the fact of her existence, and the emotional world I had imagined would automatically accompany it, a world in which I would as automatically be included. Pregnancy begins to seem to me more and more of a lie, a place populated by evangelicals and moralists and control-freaks, a place haunted by crazies with their delusions of motherhood. Or perhaps it is the clinical, hospital-appointed nature of the birth itself that has caused me to lose the thread of things, for in truth my experience of birth was more like the experience of having an appendix removed than what most people would understand by 'labour'. Without its connecting hours, the glue of its pain, the literalness of its passage, I fear that I will not make it to motherhood; that I will remain stranded as someone who merely had an operation, leaving the baby with no more sense of how she came to be here than if she had been left on the doorstep by a stork.

My physical possession of a child is, nevertheless, compelling; or rather, the physical fact of her remains a surprising embodiment of my feelings of emptiness. These sensations do not belong to my voided and sutured body. I have felt them before, throughout my life: a yearning for some correspondence with an object outside myself, a yearning to have, to experience otherness through ownership. As yet these yearnings, and their satisfaction by the object of the baby, are not so distinct from material cravings. The baby, after all, is a doll whom I dress and feed and carry about as proudly as a little girl. These libations are modest, but the premium of their object is high. Other possessions have faded in their interest, or have suffered from my irresponsibility or the changing fashions of my desire. Now I am held in a kind of stasis of expectation and unstated commitment as I wait to discover the complexity of what I have. My certainty that this complexity will show itself, and that when it does I might well be unequal to it, occasionally fades and is forgotten as the baby sleeps and feeds and silently stares. She is pale and pretty and tiny. Other people exclaim at her goodness. I am, apparently, her mother.

When she explodes, rather later but no less spectacularly than the midwife predicted, I am caught languid and somewhat unprepared in the pleasant rays of my false dawn. I have taken her for a walk in the park with a friend. I am, I believe, being rather successful: walking, talking, while the baby sleeps on in a pouch against my chest. In the two or so weeks since her birth I appear to have soldered together my past and present, to be both myself and a mother. I have physical contact with my child. I talk to my friend. I decide to risk this vision by taking us all to a café on the other side of the park, where I must remove the baby from her pouch and sit with her on my lap at a table and drink coffee. The perturbation I feel while contemplating and then executing this feat belongs, as does my vision, to a dream: it is the feeling that will press against and then puncture my sleep, letting in the first rivulet of consciousness and behind it the raging flood of the real. The fact is that I know neither what it is to be myself nor to be a mother. I know neither my child nor my friend. I don't even know about the weather. We sit at an outside table. A bruised bank of cloud gathers over us. It starts to rain, hard. I try to pack the baby back into her pouch, and I do it clumsily and unconfidently, and suddenly she starts to cry, to scream with an extraordinary, primitive anguish; and I am in disarray, knocking over coffee cups, fumbling with change, trying to speak, to pacify, to explain, holding the baby this way and that in the drenching rain and finally running through the park, the empty pouch flapping at my front, the roaring baby held out before me like something on fire, my friend trotting embarrassed behind, until we reach the road and madly, desperately, I flag down a taxi and somehow force the chaos of us into it. I'll call you soon, says my friend strangely. I glimpse her through the window, slim and well-dressed, compact, somehow extraordinarily demanding and utterly implacable, politely waving from the pavement. A feeling of social anxiety, of terrible, private unease dogs me on the way home as I fight in the swaying taxi to stem my daughter's grief, the breathtaking geyser of it as if from somewhere deep and dark and without limit. These two trains of thought do not disturb each other. I am surprised to discover how easily I have split in two. I worry; I console. Like a divided stream, the person and the mother pay each other no heed, although moments earlier they were indistinguishable: they tumble forwards, each with its separate life, driven by the same source but seeking no longer to correspond.

The vision of myself that I briefly glimpsed in the park – unified, capable, experiencing 'the solidarity of life' – is one that I will continue to pursue over the coming months. It proves elusive. Its constituents, resolutely hostile, are equally unruly. To be a mother I must leave the telephone unanswered, work undone, arrangements unmet. To be myself I must let the baby cry, must forestall her hunger or leave her for evenings out, must forget her in order to think about other things. To succeed in being one means to fail at being the other. The break between mother and self was less clean than I had imagined it in the taxi: and yet it was a premonition, too; for later, even in my best moments, I never feel myself to have progressed beyond this division. I merely learn to legislate for two states, and to secure the border between them. At first, though, I am driven to work at the newer of the two skills, which is motherhood; and it is with a shock that I see, like a plummeting stock market, the resulting plunge in my own significance. Consequently I bury myself further in the small successes of nurture. After three or four weeks I reach a distant point, a remote outpost at which my grasp of the baby's calorific intake, hours of sleep, motor development and patterns of crying is professorial, while the rest of my life resembles a deserted settlement, an abandoned building in which a rotten timber occasionally breaks and comes crashing to the floor, scattering mice. I am invited to a party, and though I decide to go, and bathe and dress at the appointed hour, I end up sitting in the kitchen and crying while elsewhere its frivolous minutes tick by and then elapse.

The baby develops colic, and the bauble of motherhood is once more crushed as easily as eggshell. The question of

what a woman is if she is not a mother has been superceded
for me by that of what a woman is if she *is* a mother; and of
what a mother, in fact, is.

Colic and Other Stories

My daughter has colic. Horses, I was of the opinion, had colic. It seems a callous appellation for what afflicts her, the wordless suffering of babies and beasts. I am sure there must be a word for it in German, something compound like *lifegrief* that would translate as *outpouring of sorrow at the human condition*, for I do not entirely believe that it is a digestive malaise. Nor, I suspect, does the medical profession: I see it referred to variously as three-month colic, 'colic', and 'what many people understand by the term "colic"'. Occasionally a brutal practitioner will call it 'wind', hinting at a view of emotion in children as pestilential and unsavoury. All, however, agree that it presents itself as bouts of apparently causeless crying which occur at specific times of the day and for which there is no cure or consolation.

My daughter's symptoms correspond exactly to this description, save for some confusion over the times at which the colic occurs, which seem not specific but general, random and frequent. I consult books on the subject, all of which insist that colic, like a Swiss train, arrives and departs on time. My experience of the regularity of hours and days and seasons has altered so dramatically over the past few weeks that time has become a sort of undifferentiated mass ordered only by the exigencies of the baby's sleeping and waking, her crying and equally baffling contentment. The idea of her displaying a particular behaviour 'in the afternoons', as the books suggest, or 'between four and six o'clock' is outlandish. The books advise walking up and down with the baby, rhythmic rocking, putting her in a pouch or sling, singing or dancing. I have recently read that the government is providing underprivileged teenaged girls with dolls that wet their nappies and cry incessantly, in the attempt to acquaint them with the realities of motherhood. The suggestion is that these dolls will rain down upon the pavements from the top floors of tower blocks within an hour of their issue, leaving the girls free to pursue careers in high finance. My books, similarly, carry health warnings on the subject of crying. A baby's crying, I am told, can cause depression and psychosis, and can result in you harming your baby. If you feel that you would like to harm your baby, put it in a safe place and leave the room for ten minutes. The tone of this instruction is curt, following on from mellifluous pages on the subjects of breastfeeding, bonding, and how you and your partner might divert yourselves sexually until you are able to resume what is described as 'full intercourse'. It peters out into a series of telephone numbers, for organisations with names like CRY-SIS.

Having apparently reached a sort of Land's End of charted motherhood, I quickly see that the problem is one I must study and solve myself. *Mothers soon come to recognise the meaning of their baby's different cries*, I read. I have indeed worked out that on those occasions when the crying is halted by feeding, I might interpret in retrospect its meaning to have been that of hunger; or one of its meanings, in any case. The baby's cries are so deafening, so urgent, so redolent of emergency that my first instinct on hearing them is always to rush her to hospital, or leave the building as if a fire alarm were going off. I understand that crying, being the baby's only means of communication, has any number of causes, which it falls to me, as her chief companion and link to the world, to interpret. Further, it is suggested to me that this interpretation is being used as the information upon which she is with every passing minute founding the structure of her personality. My response to these early cries, in other words, is formative. I should do nothing that I don't intend to continue doing, should make no false moves, lest I find myself co-habiting in the months and years to come with the terrible embodiment of my weaknesses, a creature formed from the patchwork of my faults held together by the glue of her own apparently limitless, denatured, monstrous will.

I have no difficulty in understanding what I read of the early relationship between mother and child. The child's yearning to be repossessed by the mother's body, its discovery of desire and satisfaction, its exploration of the limits of itself, and of another person and the fact of that person's own will; the mother's impulse both to protect and to expose, to yield and to separate, her responsibility both to love and to sort of steer everything in the right direction: I can see it all. The problem is that this vision doesn't much seem to resemble my situation. The baby's objections seem both comprehensive and startlingly personal; my own responses random, off-key and profoundly unmagical. It is not only difficult to believe that I am the object of the baby's desire, an object she is unresting in her attempts to enslave to her own will; it is in fact quite possible that she doesn't like me at all. I have enough imagination to picture the blur of her world, the fog of herself through which differentiation is impossible, the imperatives of her body and yet its paralysis; I do not believe that she is necessarily composing a list of objections to my conduct. It is merely that when I come looming through this fog I don't appear to improve things.

I wake to find her red and rigid on the bed beside me, the room vibrating with sound. It is 9.30 am. I have been up many times in the night to feed her, and at some late point we clearly slumped jointly into an unexpected sleep. Other people have gone to work, to school, while we slept: the world is at its desk. We are in the housewifely slurry of everything that is both too late and too early, of madness and morning television. The day lies ahead empty of landmarks, like a prairie, like an untraversable plain. The baby is roaring. It is the sort of sound that permits no pause between deep sleep and full activity. I leap to my feet, pick her up and am pacing the reeling room with her within seconds. Dimly I remember feeding her perhaps two hours earlier, but decide to feed her again anyway while I think of something else I can do. My thoughts have become rat-like and rudimentary with guesswork, with lack of sleep. Feeding is something I do with a measure of confidence only because I have done it several times before, not because I understand particularly when and how it should be done. This morning she won't feed. Suddenly it is like trying to feed a kitchen appliance, or a shoe, bizarre and apparently inappropriate. Her body is ramrod-straight, her open mouth a furnace of noise, her face blue and red with fury. Milk runs in untasted rivulets down her affronted cheek. I decide on a change of scene. We go to the bathroom, where I intend to change her nappy. Again, this strategy has worked before, although I am unsure why. I lie her down on the mat. Immediately the crying stops. Delighted at the speed with which I have disarmed her, I sit down on the bathroom floor and lean back against the wall. I trill at the baby as she lies there watching me. Presently I change her nappy. I pick her up. Immediately she roars. I put her down again. She stops. I clean my teeth, I get into the bath, I get out. I get dressed. I try picking her up again in the hope that something has changed, but it hasn't. She roars. When I put her down, she stops. I wonder whether it is possible to spend the whole day in the bathroom. The telephone rings in the next door room and I go to answer it. Back in the bathroom, she roars. I turn on my heel and go back in. I pick her up. She stops.

Downstairs in the kitchen I prepare and eat breakfast with one arm while holding her with the other. She looks around happily enough as she is waltzed from cupboard to table. I read the newspaper. I clear up, again with one arm. The arm that is holding the baby has started to ache, but the consequences of a transfer to the other side are potentially devastating. Presently I see that it is time for her to be fed. Having abandoned feeding as a strategy, I am reluctant to introduce it again. At some point, though, she will grow hungry and cry, and in any case my memory of the earlier crying has become fuzzy. The idea of taking some sort of initiative, of being a mother as opposed to a rapid response unit, is attractive. Offers of milk, this time, are accepted. In the silent kitchen we sit, the baby watching me with bead-bright, unfathomable eyes as she feeds, I watching her as one would watch some exotic, uncaged animal, wondering what she is going to do next. I pray for this stasis to continue, for the telephone and doorbell not to ring, for the city to go about its morning without troubling me. It is in such moments that a drop of confidence wells glittering from the baby and slowly splashes into the gaping vessel of myself.

Her eyelids begin to droop. The sight of them reminds me of the possibility that she might go to sleep and stay that way for two or three hours. She has done this before. The prospect is exciting, for it is when the baby sleeps that I liaise, as if it were a lover, with my former life. These liaisons, though always thrilling, are often frantic. I dash about the house unable to decide what to do: to read, to work, to telephone my friends. Sometimes these pleasures elude me and I end up gloomily cleaning the house, or standing in front of the mirror striving to recognise myself. Sometimes I miss the baby and lie beside her crib while she sleeps. Sometimes I manage to read, or work, or talk, and am enjoying it when she wakes up unexpectedly and cries; and then the pain of moving from one life to the other is acute. Nevertheless, watching her eyelids droop, my excitement at the prospect of freedom buzzes about my veins. I begin manically to list and consider things I might do, discarding some ideas, cherishing others. Her eyelids droop again and close altogether. In repose her face is as delicate, as tranquil as a shell. As I look, an alarming colour spreads rapidly over it. The skin darkens, promising storms. Her eyes flip open, her body writhes, her small mouth opens like a yawning abyss of grief and pain. She roars. She bellows. She cries out in anger, agony, outrage, terror. I feel as if I have been discovered in some terrible infidelity. My thoughts of freedom cover themselves and scatter and I am filled with fury and shame.

Have I poisoned her? The idea that there was *something in the milk* always occurs to me at such times. I have seen the phrase arrayed in bullet points, stamped out in bold, in the many leaflets and books I have perused on the subject of colic. It is a terrible phrase. It fills the heart with hopelessness and gloom, like stories of corruption in high places. How will I know? How will I root out the evil? Bottle-feeding mothers are generally advised to change the baby's brand of formula milk without delay if such a suspicion adheres to them. Breastfeeders like myself must go through a rather more ascetic process of expiation. *Think back over what you've eaten and drunk over the past twenty-four hours*, I am advised. The suspects are legion, but the proof of their guilt is vague. 'Culprits', as they are called, include alcohol, coffee and chocolate; cabbage, onions and garlic; citrus fruits and spicy food. Beans. Tea. Anything raw. *Some mothers find that excluding dairy products entirely from their diet improves things somewhat.* I have been told of a woman who would use a breast-pump to remove all the milk from her breasts after she had eaten *anything*. The baby is choking and pulling her knees convulsively up to her chest. I imagine the corruption of myself running through her tracts, into her veins and recesses. I long to withdraw my sting from her innocent body. I think for the thousandth time how much I dislike breastfeeding. I want to stop. And yet the memory of the earliness, the unnaturalness of her birth always persuades me to extend her lease on my body a little longer. I am unable to decide whether the symbolic value of this offering outweighs the fact that it appears to have the effect of three-hourly administrations of cyanide.

The health visitor pays us a visit. In the hall she sniffs the air. It seems that she is investigating the house for signs of cigarette smoking. The baby's episode of colic has now concluded, a victory secured, after two hours of walking up and down the stairs, by her chancing to glimpse herself in the hall mirror. We have been standing in front of this mirror for some forty minutes by the time the health visitor arrives. She runs red talons through the baby's feathery hair and the baby flinches. She is so dainty, says the health visitor. Is she good? Yes, I snap. Presently I admit that she cries quite a lot. I am furious to have made this admission, but my search for the cure for colic is now so preoccupying that I cannot neglect the possibility that the woman might possess it. She looks at me sharply, like a bird. Are you feeding her? she says. I realise that she is talking about breastfeeding. Her reluctance to utter the word 'breast' is clear. I say that I am. In that case it will be something in your milk, she says. Oh, I say. Yes, she is *very* dainty, she continues, stroking the baby's head until I begin to worry that she will wear a patch of it away. Very dainty and *small,*

67

isn't she? How much does she weigh? I tell her. She requests the baby's growth chart. I show it to her. She examines it in silence. Your baby is failing to thrive, she informs me presently. She runs a red nail over the short, plotted line of my daughter's life. It isn't exactly vertical, I admit, but it isn't doing a u-turn back to the womb either. She has colic, I say tearfully. It's difficult for her to eat. You must feed her with formula milk, commands the health visitor. Begin by offering her a bottle after each feed and within two weeks she will have made the switch entirely. I am astonished by this advice, having laboured under the belief – and indeed under its strictures – that breastfeeding was the religion of the health services. Don't you normally advise building up the milk supply when the baby is gaining inadequate weight?, I inquire. I am, if nothing else, well informed. Your baby is failing to thrive, repeats the woman. You risk damaging her brain. Do you want to have a brain-damaged baby? I feel it unnecessary to reply to this question.

The health visitor stays for a long time. The baby and I are braced, unified and silent against her. When finally she leaves I cry. The baby stares at me in amazement. I make an immediate appointment at the doctor's surgery. My baby is failing to thrive, I tell her, bursting into her office. The doctor replies that she is absolutely fine. In fact, she's *lovely*, she says. I look at the baby, who is lying on the doctor's couch kicking her legs and smiling winningly. Can I show you something? I say. I pick her up. Immediately, she roars.

I put her down again. She stops. That *is* strange, says the doctor.

I meet a woman who tells me kindly that one day, when the baby is about three months old, the crying will stop. From one day to the next, just like that. By now the fact of the baby's crying, if not its hours, has become predictable, although its causes remain unknown. She has cried in her sling on walks, in her baby carriage when I am trying to shop, on the bus, on the subway, at the houses of friends and relations, in mine and others' arms. She has cried from one end of many dark afternoons to the other, when she and I were alone in the house and there was nothing to do, or it was raining, or I was too tired to do anything but sit with her in a chair while she cried. I have given up trying to contain the crying within a vision of adult normality, of competence. I have run home with her bawling in my arms, pulling the carriage crazily behind us while people stare. I have jumped off buses in the middle of nowhere. I have bolted from cafés. I have ended telephone conversations without explanation. I have cried myself. I have shouted, making her tiny frame jump. I have sat for long evenings while her father paced the kitchen with her, offering advice. It was better when you were doing that jiggling thing, I say; or, try that thing you did the other night when you held her face down, with your other hand on her back. I have put her in a safe place and tried to leave the room, but before I could reach the door her crying has brought me back. We have even taken her to Italy, where for three days she cried beside Lake Garda while boats glided silently beneath the mountains over the pale water and the warm air was filled with the chattering of birds and children.

One evening, sitting outside in the garden in the dusk, I realise that three months have passed and that summer has come. My daughter is lying on a rug looking at the leaves above her. She wriggles and kicks her legs and laughs at things that I can't see. She has red hair and bright eyes. I know that in some inarticulate way I have over the past weeks witnessed again her birth; that the sound of her agony, her despair, was the sound of a terrible, private process of creation. I see that she has become somebody. I realise, too, that the crying has stopped, that she has survived the first pain of existence and out of it wrought herself. And she has wrought me, too, because although I have not helped or understood, I have been there all along and this, I suddenly and certainly know, is motherhood; this mere sufficiency, this presence. With every cry she has tutored me, in what is plain and hard: that my affection, my silly entertainments, my doting hours, the particular self I tried to bring to my care of her, have been as superfluous as my fury and despair. All that is required is for me to be there; an 'all' that is of course everything, because being there involves not being anywhere else, being ready to drop everything. Being myself is no compensation for not being there. And accordingly, the whole peopled surface, the occupation of my life has been swept away by her cries. That she has stopped crying I take as an indication that she judges my training to have been successful and the rank of mother attained; a signal that we can now, cautiously, get on with the business of living together.

Loving, Leaving

Poor Mary Lennox, child-heroine of Frances Hodgson Burnett's *The Secret Garden*. Born unwanted by her *distrait* Raj-socialite parents, living an isolated life amongst servants in India, she grew up bitter, unsweetened by love. Had tragedy not felled her, uprooting her and planting her in friendlier soil, she might have stayed that way.

The cholera had broken out in its most fatal form and people were dying like flies . . . Mary hid herself in the nursery and was forgotten by everyone. Nobody thought of her, nobody wanted her, and strange things happened of which she knew nothing. Mary alternately cried and slept through the hours. She only knew that people were ill and that she heard mysterious and frightening sounds. Once she crept into the dining-room and found it empty, though a partly finished meal was on the table and chairs and plates looked as if they had been hastily pushed back when the diners rose suddenly for some reason. The child ate some fruit and biscuits, and being thirsty she drank a glass of wine which stood nearly filled. It was sweet, and she did not know how strong it was. Very soon it made her intensely drowsy, and she went back to her nursery and shut herself in again, frightened by the cries she heard in the huts and by the hurrying sound of feet. The wine made her so sleepy that she could scarcely keep her eyes open, and she lay down on her bed and knew nothing more for a long time.

When she awakened she lay and stared at the wall. The house was perfectly still. She had never known it to be so silent before. She heard neither voices nor footsteps, and wondered if everybody had got well of the cholera and all the trouble was over. She wondered also who would take care of her now her Ayah was dead. There would be a new Ayah, and perhaps she would know some new stories ... The noise and hurrying about and wailing over the cholera had frightened her, and she had been angry because no one seemed to remember that she was alive. Everyone was too panic-stricken to think of a little girl no one was fond of. When people had the cholera it seemed that they remembered nothing but themselves. But if everyone had got well again, surely someone would remember and come to look for her.

But no one came, and as she lay waiting the house seemed to grow more and more silent . . . It was in that strange way that Mary found out that she had neither father nor mother left; that they had died and been carried away in the night, and that the few native servants who had not died also had left the house as quickly as they could get out of it, none of them even remembering that there was a Missie Sahib.

I am occasionally struck by the obsessive concern for the physical safety of small children which pervades any discussion of pregnancy, birth and the early years of life. From the moment of her conception my daughter became a magnet for prescription, embroiled in debate: about alcohol units, smoke-free zones and breast versus bottle, about future dairy and gluten allergies, room temperature and sleeping position, about immunisation schedules and vitamins. Even from *before* conception, in fact, when I was urged to purge and scrub my body for her future sake, to convert it from inferred hell-hole to temple. I find something unsavoury in such puritanism, as if dark thoughts were being kept at bay. I am told to sterilise everything with which the baby comes into contact. This can be achieved either by boiling it in water for *at least* ten minutes, or by soaking in sterilising solution for half an hour and then rinsing thoroughly in boiled water. The environmental consequences of such procedures are brushed aside. Maintaining the sterility of my child, my home, myself, is paramount. Germs and evil are everywhere. I overhear a conversation concerning the difficulty of safeguarding the sterility of rubber nipples as they make the perilous journey from boiling pan to mouth. Although you can't see it happen, apparently germs, or Germans as E. Nesbit called them, land by the thousand in a matter of seconds. In the supermarket I see little jars of baby food and they are like jars of processed, denatured love. It is love that is vacuum-packed and sterilised. Sealed bags impregnated with strong fragrance are provided for its disposal after use. It is love that can make no connection with other loves, with the contaminating world.

Mary Lennox, it seems, has been sterilised by *lack* of love. Her friend Dickon tells her to get some fresh air, to get outside and watch things grow, to get dirty. In the newspaper I read what claims to be a counterblast against the clean, an article suggesting that children who are not exposed to germs are in fact more vulnerable to them. The article is not a counterblast at all. It merely transposes the subject to a shriller pitch. It lobbies for the creation of cleanliness within dirt, for dirt not to be avoided but to be encompassed by, converted to sterility. Bad dirt, dirty dirt, exists on the margins of love. It suggests neglect, failure and lack of care. Obsessive precautions against bad dirt may hint, it now seems, at a certain proximity to these margins. To own good dirt is to proclaim the superiority of your care, your love; its fearlessness and flexibility, the purity of its thought and deed, its distance from hate.

D.W. Winnicott, the eccentric but revered pediatrician and psychoanalyst of the 1940s, famously proclaimed that all mothers hate their babies 'from the word go'. He didn't mean that they didn't love them; just that they hated them too. The 'good' mother is in part the projection of this hatred, sterilising away her ambivalence, her feelings of violence and displacement, keeping her urges to abandonment in tiny, vacuum-sealed jars. What's more, says Winnicott, 'the mother hates the baby before the baby can know his mother hates him.' It is a situation quivering with the possibility of cruelty, and of regret. Winnicott also thought that there was no such thing as a baby. The baby exists only as part of the mother. While the baby has no personality, and no independent existence, what is there to love, what to hate but yourself? Freud, more conventionally, wrote that 'in the child which [mothers] bear, a part of their own body confronts them like an extraneous object to which, starting out from their narcissism, they can give complete object-love'; and indeed everywhere in the culture of maternity one can see the difficult precedence of motherly emotion, its one-sidedness, the lonely fantasy of its frilly bassinets, its tiny snow-white garments, its angelic cribs and insignia of stars and teddy bears. Like a teenager in her postered room dreaming of pop stars, a new mother's love exists in the mind and in the regalia of her material devotion. I see in the evolution of this regalia the promise of the tables being turned at some future point: in the next aisle at the supermarket things with helmets and weapons and cone-shaped breasts have replaced the angels and teddy bears; packets illegible with additives filled with things that look like small road accidents or explosions have superceded the tiny, perfect jars. The extraneous object clearly gets his own back.

I ought not to be surprised at the violent contrasts that distinguish my emotion for my baby daughter, but I am. Like most people, I have been troubled by love all my life. My loves have observed the conventions first of the familial narrative, then of the romantic. I have never sought to rewrite these conventions. I have accorded with their cadences, their plot. But of this new love I am, apparently, in charge. When I think of my child I am seized by the desire to make good all my former powerlessness, to love as I would like to be loved: mercifully, completely, un-ambiguously. Her experience of this love is for the moment rather shady and unclear. I want to write it down and put it in a drawer for her, like the title deeds to something, so that she will have some proof, some inheritance, should something happen to me before I get a chance to explain it to her. The need for such an explanation asserts itself almost from the beginning, not because she is too small to understand that she is loved, but because the love itself, or at least my management of it, has a few teething difficulties of which I, being in charge, feel it necessary to give some kind of account.

One morning, when she is six weeks old, I am alone at home trying to get her to go to sleep. I am extremely tired. The night has been filled with fireworks, with surreal adventures and Olympian feats of endurance, and dawn has arrived like a hangover. She, and hence I, have not slept for many hours. For perhaps the twentieth time in ten hours I feed her and put her down in her cradle. I am not asking for a solid stretch: I merely require a few minutes to myself gluing parts of my face back on and saying things aloud in front of the mirror to see if I've actually gone mad. At this point I don't just *want* her to go to sleep. She *has* to go to sleep otherwise I don't know what will happen. My position is at once reasonable, utterly desperate, and non-negotiable. I put her firmly in her crib. I remove myself to the bathroom and close the door. There is a long moment of silence that is both blessed and threatening. It is filled with my command, and with the possibility that her requirements will not yield to mine, that she continues to exist beyond the limit of my patience, my love, my ability to own her. Then, next door, she cries. I begin to shout. I don't quite know what I am shouting, something about it being unfair, about it clearly being completely unreasonable that I should want FIVE MINUTES on my own. GO TO SLEEP! I shout, now standing directly over her crib. I shout not because I think she might obey me but because I am aware of an urge to hurl her out of the window. She looks at me in utter terror. It is the first frankly emotional look she has given me in her life. It is not really what I was hoping for.

Eventually she goes to sleep, silently, submissively, declining my help. Her withdrawal from me fills me with shame; the sleep itself, so longed for, is unbearable. I want to wake her up, proffering love. Now that she is still and quiet my love is once more perfect, and she is not even awake to see it. I drag myself to the telephone and sob. *I shouted at her,* I confess. In the end I confess it to several different people, none of whom gives me the absolution I am looking for. Oh dear, they say. Poor baby. They do not mean me. Don't worry, they say, I suppose she'll forget it. I understand that I am alone with my outburst, that I myself have moved outside the shelter of love. As a mother I do not exist within the forgiving context of another person. I realise that this is what *being in charge* is.

As time passes, I grow more and more tormented by the idea of children being unloved. My heart clenches at stories of abandonment and abuse. I weep before pictures on the news of orphans, refugees, children of war. A weekly television programme devoted to children having operations causes me to tear at the sofa with frantic nails. My compassion, my generalised human pity, has become concentrated into a single wound, a dark sore of knowing and of the ability to inflict. I realise that in love I have always considered myself to be victim rather than aggressor, that I have cherished a belief in my own innocence, in what nevertheless I have styled as a conflict, an irreconcilable struggle. Like a state benefit, love has always seemed to me something to which people have inalienable rights, a belief that is a mere mask for my terror at the possibility of being unloved. In the street I see a well-dressed woman berating a refugee who holds a baby in a bundle of cloth against her chest. *You get money from the government!* enunciates the woman, slowly and cruelly. She speaks in a loud, shrill voice that quavers with education and outrage. She wishes to be clearly understood. I hate her, and give the woman money under her nose just to spite her. To me she seems full of the self-confidence of the unloving, with their mysterious ability to withhold, to use against others the weapon of their own helplessness. Later, on my way home, the refugee importunes me again and confusedly I walk past her. It seems that it is not to love but to its lack that I am suddenly alive. I have not, in fact, become more loving, more generous, more capacious. I have merely become more afraid of love's limits, and more certain that they exist.

When the baby sleeps I intermittently read Olivia Manning's *The Great Fortune*, a novel which seems disconcertingly to be speaking to me. Harriet and Guy Pringle come as newlyweds to wartime Romania, where Guy works as a teacher at a university. The Pringles don't know much about each other, but they soon find out. Guy is diffuse, philanthropic, unmaterialistic, socially and politically committed. Harriet is private, particular, discriminating and self-protective. Their respective understanding of the notion of marriage is polarised. Guy wants to love everybody. Harriet wants him to love her. Guy wants love to be inclusive, outward-looking, general. Harriet wants it to be specific, adoring and protective. Guy spends a lot of time failing to get them a decent apartment, holding forth to students in cafés, and running around at all hours of the night helping distressed young women. Harriet spends a lot of time being unhappy and developing strong attachments to cats. Eventually she meets another man, with whom she pursues an intense friendship. One day, caught together during an air-raid, they shelter in a nearby basement, where Harriet sees an affecting vision:

> Two other people were on the basement stair: a woman and a small boy. The woman was seated with the boy on her knee. She was pressing the child's cheek to her bosom and her own cheek rested on the crown of his head. Her eyes were shut and she did not open them when Harriet and Charles came out. Aware of nothing but the child, she enfolded him with fervent tenderness, as though trying to protect him with her whole body.
>
> Not wishing to intrude on their intimacy, Harriet turned away, but her gaze was drawn back to them.

Transported by the sight of these two human creatures wrapped in love, she caught her breath and her eyes filled with tears.

She had forgotten Charles. When he said 'What is the matter?' his lightly quizzical tone affronted her. She said 'Nothing'. He put a hand to her elbow, she moved away, but the all clear was sounding and they were free to leave.

Outside in the street, he said again: 'What's the matter?' and added with an embarrassed attempt at sympathy: 'Aren't you happy?'

'I don't know. I haven't thought about it. Is one required to be happy?'

Harriet, it transpires, was unloved as a child. Her parents didn't like her much, and when they died she went to an aunt, who didn't like her much either. Her marriage to the undemonstrative Guy, made perhaps under the mis-apprehension of her lack of emotional expectation, has ensured that she will feel unloved for the rest of her life. It is to this feeling, the feeling of being unwanted, that she is drawn, and yet she displays little acceptance of it: on the contrary, she spends most of her time trying to elicit from Guy some proof that he *does* love her, and eventually dallies with the more sentimental Charles, who loves her and, more importantly, admits it. These admissions bring Harriet back full circle. Having secured them she withholds herself from Charles, both in word and deed, and is as reluctant and noncommital and distracted in her dealings with him as her own husband is with her. She can't, it is clear, help herself. Her glimpse of the woman and child on the stairs constitutes *The Great Fortune*'s most emotional moment by far, and it is tragically brief and subdued and unresolved. Nevertheless, it is evident that *that* is the love Harriet is after. Motherhood appears to her to be a way out of the labyrinth of adult emotion. Charles suddenly annoys her, mosquito-like, with his desire, his otherness, his silly constipated male questions about happiness. She wants two heads resting against each other, their physical entanglement, their silence. She wants her loneliness to be ultimately alleviated, atoned for. She can only turn away, 'not wishing to intrude on their intimacy'.

If parental love is the blueprint for all loves, it is also a re-enactment, a revision, an investigation of self-love. When I care for my daughter I revisit my own vulnerability, my primordial helplessness. I witness that which I cannot personally remember, my early existence in this white state, this world of milk and shadows and nothingness. My survival testifies to the fact that I, too, was cared for, and yet again and again I experience images of abandonment, of lack of love, unable to stop myself from pursuing ghoulish narratives of what would happen if I left her, if I went out for the day, if I failed to pick her up when she cried or refused to feed her. Having lived for so long high up in the bickering romantic quarters of love, it is as if I were suddenly cast down to its basement, its foundations. Love is more respectable, more practical, more hardworking than I had ever suspected, but it lies close to the power to destroy. I have never before remotely felt myself to possess that power, and I am as haunted by it as if it were a gun in a nearby drawer. My numberless ministrations, the ceaseless nurture that continues regardless of hour or mood or ability, are conducted in the very shadow of their neglect.

A few days after my daughter's birth I go to a concert. I bought the tickets weeks before, not expecting her to come so soon. I have difficulty walking because of my scar, and my grasp of the principles of breastfeeding is still tentative, but nevertheless I am determined to go. During pregnancy I had plenty of time to formulate stirring resolutions concerning the maintenance in motherhood of my independence and interests, fervently imagining myself at parties and gala events, skiing in the Bundeswald, reclining in Mediterranean sunsets, sitting meditatively at my desk, all the while with the baby in a sort of cartoon thought-bubble above my head. This state of mind has extended briefly into my daughter's life like a projection of rock overhanging a cliff. My mother-in-law is to hand to assist with the transaction, and appears nervous. Given that I am taking with me the baby's only known source of comfort and nourishment, her resources should things go wrong are limited. I scale down my plans and promise to return during the interval. From the phonebox halfway down the road I receive hesitant but favourable reports. At the tube station, too, things appear to be holding steady and I get on the train. As the stations pass I feel slightly wild with a mounting sense of wrongdoing, as if I had stolen something, and when I arrive I hobble up the escalators and fall upon the nearest telephone as if it were an oxygen mask. When I get through, the station foyer immediately fills with the tinny, bleating sound of my daughter's cries. My mother-in-law's voice comes faintly through the static and the sound of crying, strained but emphatic, as if she were filing a dispatch from a war zone. She started crying about ten minutes ago, she reports, but it seems to help if I let her suck my finger. In the street outside the traffic honks and roars. People mill around me, passing out into the London night. They are not only ignorant of the strife-torn region in which now I live; they are as remote from it as if it lay on the other side of the world. Should I come home? I shout into the receiver. It's up to you, comes the reply after a pause, I imagine she'll go to sleep eventually. I promise to phone again in five minutes' time from the concert hall. When I do, the news is bad. I rush deliriously home in a taxi, having bizarrely gone out for the evening in order to visit phone boxes in the West End. My mother-in-law's lot was no better. She came all the way to London to sit with my crying, hungry child while I telephoned her incessantly.

It is not love that troubles me when I leave the baby, like

a rope and harness paid out behind me wherever I go. It is rather that when I leave her the world bears the taint of my leaving, so that abandonment must now be subtracted from the sum of whatever I choose to do. A visit to the cinema is no longer that: it is less, a tarnished thing, an alloyed pleasure. My presence appears almost overnight to have accrued a material value, as if I had been fitted with a taxi meter, to which the price of experience is inseparably indexed. When I am out I am distracted by its ticking. My friends, whilst glad to see me, cannot necessarily afford me. We meet at the uncrossable border between the free world and the closed regime of motherhood. Though I have for the moment forgotten them, such divisions existed, of course, in the life I knew before. I have spent many evenings with people who were haunted by undone work, by unhappy relationships, by lack of money, by practical anxiety or grief. I have felt their restlessness, their fever, have seen things prowling behind their eyes. The difference lies in the matter of valour, for while it is easy to encourage your friend bravely to throw off the bonds of her anxiety, to forget her troubles and hope for better things, no one is going to cheer a mother's recovery from feelings of responsibility for her child. Instead the baby lies at home like some unintelligible goddess, luminous, pulsing, strange, an icon of lofty requirement. As her disciple I cannot but appear to have undergone some mystic conversion which distances me from those I love. I must go back to her as to something other people don't understand, and respectfully, concernedly, they let me go.

In *Madame Bovary,* Emma Bovary sends her baby daughter to live with a wet-nurse outside the town for the first few months of her life. Emma's love is roving, restless. It resists confinement in her child, in her home. Her youth and beauty have known only the cage of domesticity, the bored isolation of rural France, the rudimentary, doting love of her father and then her husband. To love her baby in turn would be to proclaim the limit of herself. Emma's urge to experience, to be the subject, the centre, draws the life out of her meanings for other people. She simply can't stand still. As a wife she is a spectre, as a mother an absence. Who, she thinks, can blame her? Her own mother is dead; she has no debt to repay. She spends her life digging tunnels underneath her marriage, an occupation to which her child brings the threat of sabotage. Like a double, a baby can inhabit its mother's loves, engaging unwanted affections, disrupting others, speaking on her behalf when her back is turned. Motherhood for Emma Bovary is an alias, an identity she occasionally assumes in her career as an adulterer. She is the essence of the bad mother: the woman who persists in wanting to be the centre of attention. At one point she tries to breathe some sincerity into the maternal role, perhaps thinking that it will save her from herself, and goes into immediate and precipitate decline:

She fetched Berthe home from the wet-nurse's. Felicite would bring her down when there were visitors, and Madame Bovary would undress her to display her legs. She adored children, she said: they were her consolation, her delight, her mania. She hugged her daughter to an accompaniment of lyrical transports . . . Emma grew thinner, her cheeks lost their colour, her face became longer. It was as though she were passing through life with scarce an earthly contact, as though her forehead bore the signature of some predestined blessedness . . . But her heart was filled with greed, rage and hatred.

When the violence fomenting within this outward saint erupts, it is upon her child that it is visited.

The fire was out, the clock ticked on. She was struck with a vague wonder that outward things could be so calm when all her being was in turmoil. Between the window and the work-table, baby Berthe, in her little knitted boots, moved uncertainly, trying to reach her mother and cling to her apron-strings.

'Leave me alone!' exclaimed Emma, pushing her away.

But a moment later the little girl was back again, this time pressing against her knees, and staring up at her with large blue eyes, while a dribble of clear saliva ran down her chin on to her silk bib.

'Leave me alone!' the young woman said again in a sudden access of irritability.

The expression of her face frightened the child and she started to cry.

'Oh, do get *away!*' cried her mother, elbowing her aside.

Berthe stumbled against the foot of the chest-of-drawers, and fell, cutting her cheek against one of the brass ornaments. The blood began to flow.

Berthe, she of the little knitted boots and the displayed legs, grows up unloved, Flaubert tells us. After the deaths of her parents, she is sent to earn her living in a cotton mill. She is her mother's blighted product, her abandoned project. She does not bear the hallmark, the authoritative stamp of maternal love. She fades away into the darkness.

It is only much later that I realise that my daughter is embarked on her own career in love, has already begun what will probably be the greatest of all the stories of her life. When did she start? How did she learn? When did love pass over her, leaving its imprint like the ghostly emanation of frost, issuing its secret invitation to the ball? Emotion lived in her, nameless, untamed, from the very start: I heard its bellows and shrieks, its purrs of satisfaction. But as her being strives towards civilisation, so this emotion begins to take forms. When she is nine months old her father and I go away for a week without her, and when we come back she does not evince pleasure or surprise or even anger, but for some minutes silently passes herself from his arms into mine and back again, over and over, like water being poured from one vessel into another: and I realise that by going away we have made her lose her shape, that with both of us gone she has lost that which contained her. By the time she is a year old she has learned to love, as she is learning to act and to speak, primitively but recognisably. She loves like a butterfly or a hummingbird, briefly bestowing herself hither and thither, zig-zagging about her doting world with the irrefutable logic of pure impulse. She has learned to walk and hence to select, to flatter, running towards a loved one, throwing her short arms around a desired object in embrace, placing her small, motionless lips here and there in imitation of a kiss. We who have loved her unacknowledged for all these months are delighted. She has learned to spurn, too, to prefer. '*Da!*' she sobs histrionically if I pick her up at an inappropriate moment. 'Ma,' she asseverates coquettishly when she senses my interest beginning to wander.

It is in some ways profoundly relieving, the development of her preferences and moods, the slow emergence, like another birth, of her character. Her self, for so long a mystery we attempted to solve, a space we filled with guesses, is taken from us like a worrying charge. Now she has arrived to claim herself, to take herself from us, and this separateness marks the end of one kind of love and the beginning of another. The one-sided passion of her infancy, that ferment of terror and responsibility, that dark flood of undifferentiated emotion, has subsided. It was love for an object, love in the mind, at once everything and nothing. I no longer find myself swept along by the waves of generalised human pity or grief that washed back and forth over the defenceless plain of my heart. This new love is banked and dammed. It is love with walls, with rooms. It is conversational, corresponding, detailed, civilised. It is more like romantic love, the love of adults, than I could have anticipated. I have to stop myself from talking about my daughter, from recounting her exploits and narrating her relation to me. There is less that I have to do for her now, and the withdrawal of her helplessness draws a veil over the murky history of my care of her. I imagine, ashamed, her caring for me when I am old, bringing the bedpans and the bottles; and I wonder what I will have scored, what undisclosed quantity of loyalty and love I have earned during these testing months. I did not know, in truth, that they were a test. I forgot that she would one day spring to life, would one day walk and talk and tell me what she thought of me. I wonder if I offended her with my reluctance, my fury. I wonder if I tormented her. I hope that I have been good, like Cinderella, when it was hard to be; not like the ugly sisters with their big feet and horny toes, whom retribution has unforgiving in its sights, who love, but too late.

Motherbaby

One day I notice that my daughter has a faint line, like a join, running from the top of her head directly down the centre of her body. It looks like the place where the two halves of her were glued together, and gives her the worrying appearance of being hand-made. During pregnancy I too developed such a line, a seam bisecting the globe of my stomach as if in preparation for some cosmic knife to cut me precisely in half. This line, the *linea negra*, is a common feature of pregnancy: it has a medical explanation which is nonetheless overshadowed by its atmosphere of symbolism, its prophetic bearing. My daughter's line eerily compliments my own, as if I had been taken apart and reassembled into two people.

I read somewhere that it is inappropriate to refer to a mother and her newborn child as two separate beings: they are one, a composite creature best referred to as mother-and-baby or perhaps motherbaby. I find this claim unnerving, even threatening, in spite of the fact that it perfectly describes the profound change in the co-ordinates of my being that I experience in the days and weeks after my daughter's birth. I feel like a house to which an extension has been added: where once there was a wall, now there is a new room. I feel my heat and light flowing vertiginously into it.

Motherbaby is designed to be an entirely sustainable unit. The baby is born installed with the ability to suck. The mother, meanwhile, has received notice during pregnancy of a Change of Use. Her breasts are requisitioned, deprogrammed: work is carried out on glands, on tissues. By the time the baby comes they are like two warheads on red alert. The baby sucks; the machinery springs into action; milk is magically produced. This milk is entirely sufficient to feed the baby for the first six months of her life, until she is able to sit up and eat food. It is designed to give the baby every nutrient she might need. It is sterile and emerges at the correct temperature. It can be given anywhere and at any time. As the baby grows, the mother shrinks. The reserves of fat she accumulated during pregnancy fuel the work of the breasts. Her uterus contracts; hormones circulate and are discharged. Her body is writing the last chapter of the story of childbirth. It has the beauty, the symmetry, of a dance. By its end, motherbaby is ready for life as mother and baby. The paint has dried; the joins no longer show. Ingenious, no?

Do you want to try putting her to the breast? the midwife

enquires as I am wheeled from the operating theatre. I look at her as if she has just asked me to make her a cup of tea, or tidy up the room a bit. I still inhabit that other world in which, after operations, people are pitied and looked after and left to recuperate. My daughter's small body, bundled in blankets, is handed to me, and as I take her I experience a moment of utter, almost visionary, clarity. In this moment I realise that a person now exists who is me, but who is not confined to my body. She appears to be some sort of colony. What she needs and wants will vie with, and often take priority over, what I need and want for the foreseeable future. I put her to the breast. The word 'natural' appears in a sort of cartoon bubble in my head. I do not, it is true, feel entirely natural. I feel as though somebody is sucking my breast in public.

The midwife compliments my daughter on her sucking. She is territorial and confident. She knows how to suck better than I know how to be sucked. Bizarrely, I imagine this fact to be the result of some prenatal conspiracy, in which my body was named as the pick-up point. *The milk will be in the breast. The midwife will give the signal. You must take the milk every three hours otherwise the supply will dry up. Our agents will be in touch shortly. They will come to the woman's house calling themselves 'health visitors'.* After perhaps a quarter of an hour of sucking a vestige of my assertiveness rises to the surface like something from a shipwreck. I need a cup of tea, to wash, to rest. I realise that while the baby is feeding I can do none of these things. I wonder when she will stop. Eventually I drift into a half-sleep and when I awake I see that detachment has occurred. My daughter lies in my arms with her mouth open and her eyes shut, giving nothing away. The next time we do it I find that I have acquired an awareness of the matter of stopping. I sit there for what seems to me to be a reasonable amount of time, and then I wait. I watch her pink pursed lips, her jaw moving up and down, trying to detect in them some hint of finality. I shift about meaningfully. I look around the room hoping that by the time I look back stopping will somehow have been achieved. Another fifteen minutes pass, then half an hour. Finally, for no apparent reason, her mouth releases the nipple with a self-possessed pop. This pop seems to me to punctuate a decision in which I played no part. Just put your little finger in her mouth and force her gums open, says the midwife cheerfully when I tell her the next day that I have been feeding the baby for an hour and believe that my legs have gone into deep paralysis. I am delighted with this advice, which I receive like a mandate for my own continuance. I am allowed to live, it seems. My daughter's eyes are shut. I put my finger into the corner of her mouth and silently wrench it open, like a prisoner attempting a jailbreak.

Back at home, the slow-moving bulk of motherbaby wanders the fragile rooms, as brainless and clumsy as a dinosaur. Milk drips unbidden from my breasts, soaking my clothes. Small daggers of pain prick my body. I cohabit uneasily with myself, with the person I was before. I look at this person's clothes, her things. I go through her memories, like an imposter, prurient and faintly scandalised. Her self-involvement, her emotional vulnerability alarm me. I inhabit her loves, her concerns, with the detachment of a descendant piecing together family history, with the difference that these concerns still live: I am importuned by them; they require my involvement. Love, expectation, anger and resentments flow in their accustomed channels towards me and though they fill me with a strange aversion I struggle to contain them, to avert disaster. I am like a spy, bent upon the maintenance of an outward appearance while my existence revolves covertly around the secret of my daughter. I long to talk to other spies, to unburden myself to them. When I meet women who have children the truth spills indiscreetly from my mouth. I don't care about myself, I say. I have no subjectivity. They could do anything to me and I wouldn't care.

Threads of association hang from me, as if I were unravelling, entangling themselves in the world's weakness. I see elderly people, people in wheelchairs, people begging for money or crying in the street, and they tug at my fibres: I feel I should provide for them, should gather them up, should put them to the breast. *Breastfeeding mothers must remember to take good care of themselves*, a hospital leaflet informs me, *and should drink an extra liter of fluid each day, at least some of which should be milk*. I cannot drink. The story of my need is over. I believe myself to be immune, with the immunity of a dead thing, to everything I once felt so deeply. Instead I have become a responsive unit, a transmitter. I read that my daughter is receiving my antibodies, my resistance, through my milk and sometimes I imagine I can feel it flow out of me like a river of light. I imagine it lining the little hollow of her body, strengthening her walls. I imagine my solidity transferring itself to her, leaving me unbodied, a mere force, a miasma of nurture that surrounds her like a halo.

The feeding goes on for hours. In the old days, I am informed, women breastfed their babies for strictly twenty minutes every four hours. They weren't 'allowed', they say, to do anything else. Those who adhered to it were, I imagine, delighted with this imaginary prohibition. It has a sort of Marxist appeal, and hence has since been discredited. The modern regime is all supply and demand. It recommends feeding the baby whenever she is hungry, by which means the breasts will produce the amount of milk she wants. You may be surprised by how hungry she is; you may find yourself feeding her twenty or thirty times in twenty-four hours, but don't worry! *It is impossible to over feed a breastfed baby.* This last claim suggests to me that feeding is entirely meaningless. I leaf through books on the subject looking for some mention of myself, some hint of concern for me as I sit pinioned twenty to thirty times a day in my armchair, but there is none. I begin to feel like a stretch of unprotected wilderness, ringing with the shriek of chainsaws, the drill of oil wells. Even the glimmer of hope offered me in the hospital is snatched away. In spite of the midwife's assurance the practice of timing or limiting feeds is, I learn, frowned upon. If you end the feed yourself, how will you know whether she's had enough? The customer, it seems, is always right. Something in the science of all this disturbs me. How often should I feed her, I ask another midwife when she comes to the house. Whenever she's hungry, replies the midwife. How do I know when she's hungry? You'll soon be able to tell, she replies with a glint that I think is meant to be conspiratorial. But in the meantime, I persist, how do I know? The midwife looks worried. It is clear that I have a problem. She gives me the details of a breastfeeding clinic run by the hospital. Her handwriting is round and cheerful as a child's.

The clinic is in a large room on the top floor of the hospital. When I open the door I am hit by a wave of noise. The room is packed. Women are sitting on the floor, on tables, two to a chair. Above the ferment of their conversation the sound of crying babies rises like a dissonant chorus of sirens. The air is hot and clammy with waiting, with noise. A woman with a clipboard fights her way through the crowd to take my details. Don't feed the baby until you've seen one of the midwives, she says. Alarmed, I ask her how long this will be. She laughs benignly and says that as I can see they are quite busy today. She does not appear concerned that the exigencies of her clinic are expected to unseat the volatile rule of motherbaby. I find a space on the floor and sit down on it with my daughter in my lap.

The other women talk and laugh loudly. Their faces are flushed with the room's heat. They manhandle their babies distractedly, turning them this way and that, putting fingers or dummies in their mouths. They flail and grizzle, their red little faces peevish as the faces of old men. Bonnets and booties and mittens on strings fly from agitated limbs. The babies boil like a row of angry kettles. When they cry, the mothers talk louder. One woman shouts into her mobile phone. Now and again a door on the far side of the room opens and a name is called. My daughter stares with round, startled eyes. She appears disarmed by this gathering of her kind. I wonder why we are all here, and then remember that it is because we are having problems breastfeeding. I find this difficult to believe: the happy, hub-like atmosphere of the room has drained feeding of its significance. The babies cry and complain, but the women have lashed themselves together to form a raft of comradeship and they sail merrily over that which separately would have drowned them. I begin to see my problems as those of isolation, of estrangement from the world. By the time my name is called I can no longer picture these problems clearly enough to describe them.

The consulting room is small and quiet. Five or six women sit in a neat row, their feet raised on piles of telephone directories, breastfeeding their babies. The babies lie regally on white pillows on their mothers' laps. Two women in white coats walk up and down the row, adjusting pillows, removing or adding a telephone directory. Occasionally they speak to one of the mothers in a low voice, and the other mothers look up, their faces as innocent and uncomprehending as moons. I am asked quietly whether I would like a cup of coffee. One of the white-coated women comes and sits down beside me. She has long grey hair and round spectacles. Beneath her white coat I glimpse the flamboyant, multicoloured fabric of her dress. Suddenly I am filled with hope, at the curableness of my situation, at the existence of this concrete expression of that which I had thought inexpressible. I am sick, and this woman is going to heal me. She asks me to tell her what's wrong. *Everything*, I want to say but don't. I find that I can fix on nothing specific to tell her. Presently I say that the baby seems to feed for an inordinate length of time. She nods her head vaguely. I sense that she is not listening. She gives me the pillow and the telephone directories and tells me to start feeding. Meanwhile she wanders off to inspect her row of motherbabies. When she comes back she adjusts my daughter's head and tells me to hold the lower half of her body higher so that she is sloping backwards. Her colleague catches sight of this manoeuvre. That's new, she cries, laughing delightedly. Why not, my woman gaily replies, gesturing extravagantly with her hands. Passing each other as they cross the room they twirl girlishly about. I begin to realise that I am not going to be cured, other than by the small possibility that these women are witches and the pillows and telephone directories the impedimenta of their sorcery. My daughter has gone to sleep. When nobody is looking I wrench her mouth open with my little finger. Feel free to come back again, the women say, waving and mouthing like hostesses, as I leave, and I walk quickly through the crowded waiting room, through the memory of the hospital's eerie corridors and down flights of echoing stairs, shrugging them off like stifling layers, desperate for the air of the outside world.

The days pass slowly. Their accustomed structure, the architecture of the past, has gone. Feeds mark them like stakes driven into virgin soil. By the time my daughter is three weeks old I have discerned in them a pattern. She cries with mysterious punctuality every three hours. I realise that where I was counting hours from the end of one feed to the beginning of the next, she, with her aversion to the notion of stopping, has been counting from beginning to beginning. I discover that this is true even if I stop the feed myself, and for a while feeding retreats like something tamed, like something dangerous sitting muzzled in the corner of my life. Time flows again through its dried-up tributaries. Although I still cannot believe that what comes out of my breasts is in any way legitimate, is qualified to sustain her through the intervals, neither the law nor the medical profession arrives at the house to intervene. Sometimes, when she has been two or more hours from the source of my body, I begin to feel a sort of elemental anxiety for her, as if she were walking a tightrope and had gone too far out, as if she could not exist for so long in time, in gravity, away from me. One day, she starts to cry an hour after I last fed her, and this evidence of her need converges with my disbelief in her self-sufficiency. I feed her. Over the next few days there is more crying, and then more. The cries seem to splinter off from themselves, like cracks from a central fissure, forging their jagged paths through silence until the whole surface of our routine is covered with them. I pour milk into these cracks as if to fill them: I feed her again and again in the hope of returning us to wholeness, to the state of not feeding. Once I feed her for almost two hours. That should do it, I think. Five minutes later she is crying again and I stare into the insatiable red cave of her mouth.

I think she's hungry, other people say when she cries, handing her back to me. I sit gloomy as a cow in the corners of rooms, on park benches, in restaurants or the back seats of cars, my shirt unbuttoned. Nowhere, it seems, am I safe from the accusation of hunger. Sometimes the baby cries even *while* she is feeding and I feel the triumphal urge to call a symposium. There! I would say to everyone. What do you say to THAT?

A woman comes to the house one day. She is researching a university study into the experiences of new mothers and wants to ask me some questions. The baby is crying and I am not feeding her only because I have got up to answer the door. Oh dear, says the woman. I wait for her to tell me that the baby is hungry but she does not. She asks me if I am exhausted. I say that I am. I recount, uncertainly, the rambling dream of feeding and crying that my life has become. She listens sympathetically. Look, she says presently, nodding at the baby, who I had momentarily forgotten was lying in my arms; she's gone to sleep. We both stare at the sleeping baby and eventually I get up and put her in her stroller, feeling certain that some magic has occurred, that this stranger whose colourless permed hair and pleasant, indeterminate face I have hardly noticed is in fact a being from another world, an apparition who has effortlessly rolled away the stone from the entrance to my life. The baby sleeps for three hours. The woman and I talk. As she leaves, she tells me that whenever the baby cries to remember to do something for myself before I do anything for her. I nod and thank her and close the door.

I attempt to unravel the tangle of crying and feeding in which the baby and I have become knotted up. She is now crying all of the time that she isn't feeding; I cannot physically feed her any more than I do. We appear to be approaching critical mass. Feeding has reached its logical limit. Feeding, I tell the baby silently, is not a substitute for living. Feeding is an overloaded socket that is growing hot and dangerous as every day the voltage passing through it increases.

In spite of all this, her weight gain is slow. It does indeed seem to be impossible to overfeed a breastfed baby, and I have certainly tried. I try to see things from her point of view. Every time she cries my breasts appear like prison warders investigating a disturbance, two dumb, moonfaced henchmen closing in on her, silencing her, administering opiates. She could be crying because she's tired, or in pain; she could be crying in the attempt to express herself; she could be crying, God knows, with surfeit, crying in order to relocate the silence of satisfaction, of content. I begin to suspect that I have presided over some kind of bureaucratic madness, wherein feeding has become the penalty for crying and hence creates *more* crying. Or perhaps there is some deeper root to the problem, some stealthy malaise plaguing the organism of motherbaby. Is my milk polluted by its passage through my unclean self? Is it carrying messages? Is the dark turmoil of what I feel being broadcast by my daughter's cries? There is, I suspect, some connection between my sense of etherealness, of non-being, and her increasingly furious and desperate assertions. I know that this curious function is meant to bring body and mind into a state of harmony unique in human experience. I know that other women derive feelings of fulfilment and well-being from breastfeeding. Why don't I?

Thoughts of bottles fill my head, pristine, final, dense with calories. Through them I imagine I can create a decoy, a third being who will break up the intensity of motherbaby. I imagine myself stealing out from behind her matronly façade. I imagine the baby and I allying ourselves against her, this *milchcow*, this feeder, revelling together rebelliously in unfettered emotion. These feelings are not commendable but they have at least some explanatory virtue. They express my desire to shed my motherly persona, a persona I cannot seem to support without injury to what I have come to know as my self. I remember reading a magazine article about people whose brains housed two or more alternative personalities; how these personalities just arrived one day, with their own thoughts and memories and impulses, and took up tenancy in a person's mind. Long arguments could occur between host and tenant; parties could be held if there were enough people in there. This is, I suppose, what is more commonly known as madness. Am I, then, going mad? If so it is a madness that has its genesis in pregnancy; it is the whole reproductive act, not just its postscript in breastfeeding, that has shaken my sanity. But I steeled myself to endure its strangeness, as one would endure pain, believing that on the day of her birth it would end. Like a dreamer who retains the knowledge that they are dreaming, and hence knows that they will not dream forever, I remained certain that the same physical process that had taken me away would return me to myself. I would cross back over the border, back into the country of myself, and I would know that I had done it as surely as the dreamer knows that they have woken up. What has now begun to alarm me is the fact that the dream is going on and on, is each day gathering to itself more of the appearance of reality.

Covertly, I go to a shop and buy bottles, sterilising tablets, tins of powdered formula milk. At home I lay them out like someone preparing to assemble a bomb. The baby is three months old: very soon she will stop crying as abruptly as if someone had flicked a switch, but I don't know that, will never know whether her crossing of this line was the slow and stately work of nature or the violent result of my own intervention. When evening comes I prepare the bottle. Her father is to give it to her, for we are advised that this treachery is best committed not by the traitor herself but by a hired assassin. I watch as he nudges her lips with the rubber nipple. She gnaws at it obligingly, wrinkling her nose. Presently she takes the hint of his persistence. This is not, as she had at first thought, a strange new game. She stares at the bottle and I see the realisation dawn. Her head snaps round and her eyes lock with mine. Her gaze is wondering and wounded. She sees that I am officiating over this crime. She begins to cry. I move to retract, to propitiate; my hand goes automatically to my shirt buttons. I am told to go upstairs and I go. I sit on the bed, tearful, a pain in the pit of my stomach. Minutes later I creep back down and peer around the corner. They are sitting in a pool of lamplight. The room is warm and silent. The baby is sucking the bottle. I rush back upstairs as if I had witnessed an infidelity.

It was, I reflected later, something of a pact with the devil. With the end of breastfeeding my sense of normality was duly returned to me, but for a while, whenever I picked her up or held her on my lap my daughter would turn her head towards my empty breast and I would feel the pang of her loss. Guiltily I would think that I had baptised her early in the eternal doctrine of human pain, of things passing, of what was loved vanishing, never to return. As for myself, that lactating, matronly spectre, that mother I so feared, went away, and in her place was just me. I was not so ample, so proprietorial, so necessary as she. Behind my breasts I was revealed to be doubtful, unconfident, unreliable. Over the weeks I noticed the baby moving towards her father like a plant towards a new source of light. I had lost one sort of authority, but perhaps another would come to take its place. I had defected from the throne of motherhood, but I liked to think I would evolve my own presidential style. Sometimes, in the afternoons, I would get into bed with her for a nap, and she would lie beside me drinking her bottle, her eyes fixed in fascination on my body. A preliminary wave of sleep would roll warmly over us. I could feel us falling together through the bright constellations of our thoughts. Even as I crossed the line into sleep I felt her cross it too; I felt her go to sleep just as when I was a child I used to feel snow falling outside my window. Later I would open my eyes to find her sleeping head on my stomach, her body curled as if in homecoming around my side, and I would lie very still, knowing that if I moved she would wake.

Extra Fox

There are books about motherhood, as there are about most things. To reach them you must pass nearly everything, the civilised world of fiction and poetry, the suburbs of dictionaries and textbooks, on past books about how to mend your motorbike or plant begonias and books about doing your own tax return. Childcare manuals are situated at the far end of recorded human experience, just past diet books and just before astrology.

It is possible, I sense, to make a specialism out of anything and hence unravel the native confidence of those you address. The more I read, the more my daughter recedes from me and becomes an object whose use I must re-learn, whose conformity to other objects like her is a matter for liminal anxiety. Most of these books begin, like science fiction, with a sort of apocalyptic scenario in which the world we know has vanished, replaced by another in whose principles we must be educated. The vanished world is the mother's own. It is the world of her childhood, and her own mother was its last living inhabitant. In those days, the story goes, mothers were told what to do by *their* mothers. The apocalypse, of unspecified cause but generally agreed to have been recent, put paid to that. Like the great library of Alexandria, a world of knowledge has gone up in flames. A chain of command has been broken. We will never know what these mothers whispered to their daughters, what secrets they handed down the years. Something about leaving babies in prams at the bottom of the garden, we think. But the point is that this is a new – in many ways a *better* – world. You are its first mother. And this is its first book.

My mother didn't tell me much about motherhood, it's true. She said she couldn't remember. None of you ever cried, she said vaguely, and then added that she might have got that wrong. She too seemed to have heard about this apocalypse. You all do it differently now, she said. She bought me a childcare manual, with a picture of an ugly baby sticking its tongue out on the cover. Every time I look at the picture it reminds me of what I thought about children before I had one, and what they thought about me. The recollection is a shock, like an unexpected glimpse in a mirror. The text inside is righteous and faintly bullying. It bristles with lists and bullet points, and with exclamation marks too, apparently denoting humour: they swim before me, mad as eyebrows, embarrassing as politicians' jokes. Their conviviality cannot conceal the dictatorial lust belonging to scientists of baby management. The authors prescribe a regime of mandatory, indiscriminate, perhaps life-long breastfeeding. There are pictures supplied, of women breastfeeding naked, in bed, in the bath, in groups and alone. There is a picture of a woman breastfeeding a girl of at least six. They are identically dressed, with long, shining blonde hair. Breastfed children, the book states, are not only healthier, longer-lived and more disease resistant than the other sort, they *may also be more intelligent.* I read this last claim several times, unable to make sense of it. As far as I know I myself was not breastfed, which may explain the problem. A quantity of evangelical fire is reserved for those tempted to sin with the bottle. There are lists, mnemonic, like the doodlings of schoolgirls, with headings such as 'Benefits of Breastfeeding' and 'Problems with Breastfeeding'. Problems with breastfeeding, I discover, are almost always the mother's fault.

1. **Baby cries after feeds.** The baby could be wrongly positioned on the breast. Check that you have got her latched on properly before you start. Think back over everything you have eaten or drunk in the past twenty-four hours and try to find out what might have upset her.
2. **Baby feeds too often.** Perhaps you are removing her from the breast too early. *She* should always end the feed, not you.

3. **Feeds take too long.** Why are you trying to hurry her? Perhaps you should check your schedule and find out why you are trying to rush through this important stage in your baby's life.

I feel hated, chastised. I feel repelled by these naked women with their pendulous breasts. The chapter on bottle-feeding has a sombre tone, an atmosphere of reprimand like a headmistress's study. This book supports all mothers, it says insincerely, not just those who breastfeed their babies. If you really feel you must bottle-feed then at least make sure that your baby doesn't miss out *too* much. Hold her close when you feed her, perhaps pressing her against your naked breast, or alternatively use a feeding tube. This is a small tube that you can tape to your breast, through which the baby can suck. It is especially helpful for mothers who have adopted a baby and are saddened by having to miss out on the experience of breastfeeding. Briefly, bizarrely, I find myself considering the use of a feeding tube, but before I know it we are on to 'Returning to Work'. Everyone, it seems, is suddenly going back to the office, except me. The breastfeeding angle is closely examined. What you do is, you take your breastpump to work, and at the times when the baby usually feeds you pump the milk from your breasts. I sense that all this pumping at meaningful hours is not just for old time's sake. At the end of the day you take the milk home and either freeze it or store it in the fridge. Then somebody gives it to the baby the next day while you're at work. It seems an awful lot of bother to me. I'm still in my dressing gown trying to work it out when they all come charging back for a final chapter on 'Having Another Baby'.

I am given another book by a friend, an old book that seems to date from before the apocalypse. This book does not mention breastfeeding. Instead it advises a practice run with the sterilising equipment before the birth, and the application of full make-up immediately after. The author recounts an incident after the birth of her first child (she's had four, all strapping boys) when she and her husband worked flat out in the kitchen for a full forty minutes getting that hungry baby his first bottle! There are no pictures of naked women here. Instead there are pictures of babies, clean as pins, wrapped in crisp white towelling as if the stork had just brought them. The mechanics of bathing, sterilising, scouring and nappy changing are dwelt on. The pristine chamber of the baby's room is toured. Nursery equipment is listed and illustrated. The baby spends a lot of time in the white depths of his crib, like something in a cloud or a casket, while his mother folds starched nappies into different shapes in a nearby room. These babies don't cry, or perhaps you just can't hear them all the way from the nursery. A tactful door is closed upon the sinful, rumpled warmth of the adult bed, its flesh, its secretions. We are crisply advised against ever taking baby into our bed, not if we want to keep our marriages, and besides, we'll have all hell to pay getting him out again! Night feeding appears to occur in the nursery, covertly, like an infidelity, while husbands slumber on unawares, but is quickly stamped out. The book ends abruptly on a series of cliffhangers and unanswered questions: is the baby ever taken out of his crib, or does he stay there silently before one day just getting up and going to school? Does the mother wear full make-up for night feeds? Is her husband, last seen alive working flat out in the kitchen on day one, dead, or just asleep?

My mother tries again, this time with more success. She gives me Dr Spock's *Baby and Child Care*. Dr Spock is engrossing on the subject of rashes. In fact he is a fund of information on most things, having appointed himself a sort of missionary to aid those inhabitants of swamps, mines and oil platforms who are mysteriously beyond the reach of the medical profession. His prose is full of danger and emergency: 'if you can't get to a doctor', 'if you're in a situation where you have to sterilise', 'if your milk supply is fading fast and you don't have access to a doctor, health nurse, or other medical professional'. Spock is a passionate advocate of doctors as the only things that stand between families and full-scale nuclear meltdown. Spock's doctors want nothing more than to know if your child's temperature is nudging three figures, if she won't eat her supper, if she has a flat rash of spots roughly three millimetres in diameter that rise and form hay-coloured crusts on the third day. Together, Spock hopes, doctors and parents will see off capitalism, consumerism and environmental catastrophe, for social change can only start in the home, with parents who defy traditional gender roles and act as domestic equals, who don't let their children play with toy guns or watch violent films, who explain their reasons and set a charitable example and what's more can identify the rash of impetigo, a red area of infection that blisters after three days and forms hay-coloured crusts and is highly contagious. Spock's babies are cheerful souls, in spite of their temperatures, their constant gastro-enteritis and chronic excrescences of the skin, in spite of the shadow of global destruction that hangs over them. They like their milk, and when the time comes they like their turnip too. They could use more fresh air than they generally get. They don't like being fussed too much by guilty working parents, by fathers full of suppressed anger, by mothers who want them to be walking before the baby next door. In their anomic, tyrannical hearts they like to know who's boss, for weakness drives them to enslave and dominate, to make fools of their parents. Spock has seen it all, parents who follow their children around the house with bowls of rejected food, who act as human zimmer frames for toddlers, who are in and out of bed like jacks-in-the-box all night fetching milk and rocking and soothing. It's only natural that a baby should have a lusty, rebellious nature:

what's important is that you sculpt it into something decent and upstanding, something civilised.

I imagine Spock in his office, at the end of the day, sitting in a black leather chair while the world grows dark outside. He is slightly Vulcan in appearance. He takes off his glasses and rubs his eyes. His head is full of his own refrain and he wonders for the hundredth, the thousandth time how he could be at once so accepted and so misunderstood, so dominating and yet so powerless. He has been fair, he's looked at it from all sides, and yet he can't seem to get this procreation-civilisation message over. In his head it is perfect, sound, complete, but on paper he is read as both permissive and oppressing, at once the man who spawned a generation of draft-dodgers and a sort of pediatric prince of darkness presiding over the nocturnal misery of helpless infants. They're all angry with him, and yet what did he ever do but try to help? Nobody has any respect for the medical profession any more, that's the problem, it's all going to pot, more bombs and guns and gas-guzzlers than ever, more spoiled babies . . .

I go to the bookshop myself and purchase *Your Baby and Child* by Penelope Leach. I am looking not just for answers now, but for a narrative that expresses the world of my daughter, that explains her to me again; for my involvement seems to have muddled her and as she grows more complex, less coherent, so like a bewildered lover I search for something to reorganise us and return us to the purity of our early days. Ms Leach appears to be just the thing. Her tone is smart but sympathetic. She has a schoolteacher's plain grasp of Freud and Winnicott, of theories of attachment and childcare trends. Like Mary Poppins, like someone in a fairytale, she is on the side of children. *This baby is a person* she crisply declares, scattering all before her. How would you like it if people just wanted you to go to sleep all the time and never talked to you? Or expected you to spend all night on your own in the dark? Or got angry when you cried and never wanted to play and kept moaning about wanting some time for themselves? *Poor babies!* Penelope Leach's prescription for misery is fun: more fun for baby, she says, is more fun for you. Have conversations! Show her the flowers, the sun, the sky! Don't keep her in that playpen, get in it yourself! She deploys case studies on the un-fun subject of night wakings. When Alison's baby wakes at 2 am, Alison sighs loudly and puts her head under the pillow in a fury. Alison, it seems, is the maternal equivalent of people who wear black hats in Westerns, and gets what she deserves. Her baby cries louder and louder, and when Alison finally drags herself out of bed to feed her, the baby is in such a state that the milk goes down the wrong way and she won't go back to sleep. Beulah, on the other hand, leaps lightly from her bed at her child's polite 2 am summons. Her baby smiles as she is lifted from her crib. She feeds gratefully and returns immediately to sleep. Alison's time score? An hour and a half, and she didn't even want to get up in the first place. Beulah's? Twenty minutes. Hah!

I try talking to my daughter. I sing her songs, rambling epics set to music in which she is the central character. She squirms with delight and makes noises back. One day she laughs, an extraordinary sound that flies from her mouth like a dove produced from a magician's hat. We all work to produce the laugh again, stumbling each time across a different formula to summon it. The baby is moved from her carriage to a chair in which she reclines against a bank of cushions like a tetchy monarch while we, her court, strive to entertain her. Her night wakings become more frequent. By day I feel a burden of social anxiety in the baby's presence, like a hostess. We await her reviews of the theatre the world has become for her. When she sleeps I read the books again until I know some of their passages by heart, and because my daughter changes but they do not their meaning never quite penetrates, the connection with the real is never made. Like schoolwork their pages refuse to spring to life and so I learn them by rote, cribbing for some assessment only I apprehend and fear.

Somebody buys my daughter a book, a cloth thing that is part-toy, and her eyes light up when she sees it. I show her the pictures. She is apparently enthralled. I buy more books for her. She can sit up now, and they surround her in stacks. She sifts through them alone, uncomplaining, for literally hours at a time while I read childcare manuals in an adjacent chair. Eventually it strikes me that there is something wrong with this arrangement. I sit her on my lap and we look at her books together; I show her the sheep, the duck, the cow. I realise that my head is full of mantras, of the maddening phrases of Spock and Leach and their ilk. Their tics have haunted me, have invaded my language. Now I point and make animal noises like someone in an asylum. Presently words begin to appear in my daughter's books and with them a new verbal virus comes to plague me. Oddly I don't mind it as much. It is inane, bizarre, redolent of madness. *Elmer flies in the wind.* I have to check it from spilling from my mouth at inappropriate times. *What's under the table, Spot?* She becomes attached to a book that is too old for her, by Dr Seuss. It is about the alphabet.

O is very useful.
You use it when you say
Oscar's only ostrich oiled an orange owl today.

There is a picture of a flamboyant ostrich holding an oil can over the head of an orange owl. Dr Spock and Dr Seuss have become confused in my mind. I imagine one became the other and these verses strike me sympathetically as the ravings of an addled sensibility, as postcards from the edge.

X is very useful if your name is Nixie Knox.

It also comes in handy
Spelling axe and extra fox.

The extra fox wears a smart yellow jacket. It haunts my dreams, flits dashingly across my waking hours.

I begin to relive at high speed my own evolution towards language, towards stories. Reading books to my daughter revives my appetite for expression. Like someone visiting old haunts after an absence I read books that I have read before, books that I love, and when I do I find them changed: they give the impression of having contained all along everything that I have gone away to learn. I begin to find them everywhere, in pages that I thought familiar: prophecies of what was to come, pictures of the very place in which I now stand, and yet which I look on with no spark of recognition. I wonder how I could have read so much and learned so little. I have stared at these words like the pots and pans, the hoarded gold of a previous civilisation, immured in museum glass. Could it be true that one has to experience in order to understand? I have always denied this idea, and yet of motherhood, for me at least, it seems to be the case. I read as if I were reading letters from the dead, letters addressed to me but long unopened; as if by reading I were bringing back the vanished past, living it again as I would like to live every day of my life again, perfectly and without misunderstanding.

*

'From the first', writes D. H. Lawrence in *The Rainbow*,

the baby stirred in the young father a deep, strong emotion he dared scarcely acknowledge; it was so strong and came out of the dark of him. When he heard the child cry, a terror possessed him, because of the answering echo from the unfathomed distances in himself. Must he know in himself such distances, perilous and imminent?

He had the infant in his arms, he walked backwards and forwards troubled by the crying of his own flesh and blood. This was his own flesh and blood crying! His soul rose against the voice suddenly breaking out from him, from the distances in him.

Sometimes in the night, the child cried and cried, when the night was heavy and sleep oppressed him. And half asleep, he stretched out his hand to put it over the baby's face to stop the crying. But something arrested his hand: the very inhumanness of the intolerable, continuous crying arrested him. It was so impersonal, without cause or object. Yet he echoed to it directly, his soul answered its madness. It filled him with terror, almost with frenzy . . .

He became accustomed to the child, he knew how to lift and balance the little body. The baby had a beautiful, rounded head that moved him passionately. He would have fought to the last drop to defend that exquisite, perfect round head.

He learned to know the little hands and feet, the strange, unseeing, golden-brown eyes, the mouth that opened only to cry, or to suck, or to show a queer toothless laugh. He could almost understand even the dangling legs, which at first had created in him a feeling of aversion. They could kick in their queer little way, they had their own softness.

One evening, suddenly, he saw the tiny, living thing rolling naked in the mother's lap, and he was sick, it was so utterly helpless and vulnerable and extraneous; in a world of hard surfaces and varying altitudes, it lay vulnerable and naked at every point. Yet it was quite blithe. And yet, in its blind, awful crying, was there not the blind, far-off terror of its own vulnerable nakedness, the terror of being so utterly delivered over, helpless at every point. He could not bear to hear it crying. His heart strained and stood on guard against the whole universe . . .

It had a separate being, but it was his own child. His flesh and blood vibrated to it. He caught the baby to his breast with his passionate, clapping laugh. And the infant knew him.

Hell's Kitchen

One day I came across two articles in the newspaper, both written by men. The author of the first had recently become a father. The tone of his article was valedictory, funereal. Its subject was the death of freedom, its untimely murder by the state of parenthood. In form it was curiously poetic: a brisk tour of the man's love for his newborn child – Oh babe, with thy pearly limbs, thy jewel-bright eye!, etc. – is quickly followed – but too late, too late – by his realisation that his custody of this gem poses a serious threat to his ability to go to New York for the weekend, as he was wont to do at this time of year to do his Christmas shopping. New life has arrived like a letter-bomb, a mere wrapping for the death of pleasure. In an imaginative passage, he tries going to New York in his mind with his wife and child, and a miserable trip it certainly is. They can't go out in the evening, shops and museums are a chore, the hours on an airplane pure torture. I shan't bother to go, he declares bitterly. He realises that eighteen years of this lie ahead of him. In New York the Christmas lights are sparkling. The shops glitter with treasure and emanate a delicious fragrance, the smell of the past, of fleeting, irrecoverable happiness. His anger, his disbelief, his sense of injustice are palpable. It is as if he has lost a limb, or been convicted of a crime he didn't commit. I imagine him sitting in a fashionable penthouse flat with his baby like a ball and chain around his ankle, surrounded by expensive purchases from the past, a droplet of regret sliding down his cheek. One gains the distinct impression that he would give the baby back immediately if he could. It is over! he howls in a final, despairing couplet. It is over! Whither youth, glamour, romance? Whither New York?

The author of the second article has three children, and so is more deadpan, more level-headed in what he has to say. He is witty, in a dry way. He has been hardened: his punch is slower in coming but more brutal when it does. He is talking about weekends. He describes, lingeringly, the Saturday morning lie-in. Drowsing, love-making, breakfast in bed. Up, finally, for a coffee and a leaf through the papers. A long bath. Then choices, choices: shopping, a long walk, a late lunch? An afternoon movie, an art gallery? More sleep? A haircut, a trip to the gym. Read a novel. Dinner with friends, the opera, a party. Sunday morning, more of the same. He wishes to know whether people who don't have children realise what weekends are like for people who do. The fact is, there *are* no weekends. What

the outside world refers to as 'the weekend' is a round trip
to the ninth circle of hell for parents. Weekends are when
children don't go to school. Weekends are when child-
minders and nannies have time off. You are woken on a
Saturday morning at six or seven o'clock by people getting
into your bed. They cry or shout loudly in your ear. They
kick you in the stomach, in the face. Soon you are up to
your elbows in shit – there's no other word for it – in shit
and piss and vomit, in congealing milk. Forget about giving
your wife a cuddle. You've got to get up and deal with shit.
Downstairs in the kitchen a storm of spilled cornflakes,
tears and television rages. More shouting in your ear. It's
raining outside. After some time both you and they seem to
have had enough – could it be lunchtime, time for a nap,
for bed? You look at your watch – it's seven fifteen. Like
everybody else you've been working all week. Like everybody else you are hungover: you were probably out last
night engaging in the usual pretence of being normal. The
world forces you to conceal these Saturday mornings like a
guilty secret. By eight forty-five it becomes clear that some
action must be taken. The question is, do you try to front it
out at home in the hope that your children will suddenly
become like children in novels, playing long imaginative
games that don't involve you, or do you give in immediately
and get in the car? You get in the car. Nothing is open yet
so you drive around, circling like a predator looking for
something to attack. It's raining. You put on a tape, a

children's tape, full of jingly music and animal noises. Such tapes have become, for you, the soundtrack of hell. In the back seat the children fight. When you get stuck in traffic, they cry. Someone is sick. Someone else wets their pants. You catch sight of yourself in the rear-view mirror: you haven't shaved, you haven't brushed your hair. You are stinking, soiled, terminally chaotic, like a sink-full of undone dishes. You and your wife are like people in a war, people trying to pilot a tank through battle. You give each other curt orders, your faces sideways. Every now and again one of you loses control and shouts violently, and when this happens the other shows no reaction. He or she has seen it all before. Neither of you has had an unbroken night's sleep in five years. You are aware, vaguely, that there must be a reason things are like this, that other people would say you'd chosen it, done it to yourself, but if that's true you certainly can't remember doing it. You are like someone wrongly in prison, someone in a Kafka novel, fielding your punishment without knowing your crime.

I think about the days people spend with their children, remote, crisis-torn, then elapsed, like the days of a disaster on the other side of the world. These days do not seem to attract the recognition, the international concern they evidently deserve. Even those parents who publicise their predicament are difficult to counsel. Besieged as they are, yet they generally disclose no contrary desire; their attitude to the glories of an unencumbered life is, if anything, faintly mocking. They rail, and yet an offer permanently to remove their children from their care would almost certainly be turned down: they vent their frustration, but keep their love a closely guarded secret. Such versions of family life come to seem impenetrable to me. I cannot subscribe to the hell they portray, not because I do not recognise it, but because the hardship of parenthood is so unrelievedly shocking that I feel driven to look deeper for its meaning, its cause. At its worst moments parenthood does indeed resemble hell, in the sense that its torments are never-ending, that its obligations correspond inversely to the desires of the obliged, that its drama is conducted in full view of the heaven of freedom; a heaven that is often passionately yearned for, a heaven from which the parent has been cast out, usually of his or her own volition. The difference lies in the possibility of virtue, and for this reason I understand better those people who would have you believe that their babies don't cry, that their children bring them only joy, that their families sit around together reading novels, quietly discussing the environment or engaged in constructive play: seeing the situation they have decided, out of pride or integrity or some obscure loyalty to themselves, to make the best of it.

What is striking, in any case, is that these dissident voices are male. Their outrage is fresh, the protest of the novice or new arrival. There is something shaming in their objections, for they have arrived in the world of childcare full of revolutionary zeal, of disgust and despair at what they see, and their expostulations, their cries for reform, vibrate with unspoken criticism of those who have lived un-protesting under its regime for so long: the lifers, the long-term residents, women. One does not, it is true, often hear a woman observe with incredulity that her baby won't seem to go away, not even for a night so that she can get some sleep, but that doesn't mean she doesn't think it, hasn't always thought it. I often think that people wouldn't have children if they knew what it was like, and I wonder whether as a gender we contain a Darwinian stop upon our powers of expression, our ability to render the truth of this subject. People without children certainly don't seem very interested in anything that people with have to say about it: they approach parenthood blithely, as if they were the first, with all the innocence of Adam and Eve before the fall. Men, it seems, are blowing our cover with their loud objections.

Women are said to observe a parturitional apartheid in their approach to conversation about motherhood, main-taining a sort of political *froideur* when drawn upon the subject by childless female friends and then exploding with gory confidences once back in the safety of their coven of co-mothers. I have observed several times an expression of polite, horrified surprise on the faces of new mothers, as if they had just opened an inappropriate Christmas present: clearly they were unprepared. The small matter of night feeding is certainly kept well under wraps. When my daughter woke and cried during her first night on earth I was quite affronted, and had not the slightest idea what to do with her. The notion of feeding came to me late, when it struck me that by putting something into her mouth I might succeed in stopping her crying. I don't think I realised I would have to do this every three hours night and day for the next year.

There is in truth no utterance that could express the magnitude of the change from woman or man to mother or father, and in the absence of definitive statement the subject becomes peopled with delusions and ghosts, with mis-apprehensions and exaggerations and underestimations, becomes separated from the general drift of human con-versation, so that parenthood is not a transition but a defection, a political act. Beginning with the object of the baby, like an unexploded bomb in a Hitchcock film its mere, unalleviated presence draws the immediate drama to itself, causes, for the people who live with it, the world to slew in its direction. It is like a social experiment, something a scientist would do: leave a baby in a room with two adults, retreat, and see what happens. The baby cries. The cry is loud and urgent, similar to the sound made by a fire alarm. The woman picks up the baby. The sound stops. When she tries to put it down again the baby cries. She holds it for a long time. The man grows bored and the woman tries to put the baby down but it cries. When the woman becomes tired she gives the baby to the man. The baby cries. The man walks around with it and it stops. The man grows tired. Both the man and the woman sit down and look at the baby anxiously. They are too tired to speak, but at least they have stopped the baby crying. They feel as if they have achieved something. It starts crying again. It cries so much that they hate it. Whenever it stops crying the relief is so great that they love it. This happens over and over again, but the experiment dictates that each time it becomes harder to find a means of stopping the baby crying. Soon it is taking all their ingenuity and energy to work it out. They are given no breaks and no assistance from the outside world is permitted. The experiment runs day and night without pause. The couple must work out for themselves who sleeps when, and this is the greatest cause of argument between them. Each feels it is unfair if the other goes out, and even going to work is considered an easy, attractive option. The experiment can be broadened by introducing more babies, and by altering laboratory conditions with the use of all or any of the following factors: progress in the baby's development from crying to rolling off tables, crawling out of windows, choking, falling over and other dangerous, attention-seeking behaviour which requires strenuous round-the-clock parental vigilance; the addition to the room of dirt, mess and endemic domestic chaos which no amount of work appears to eradicate; the occurrence, in the working partner's conversation, of

attractive, childless members of the opposite sex; and
telephone calls, erratically spaced to promote anxiety, from
members of the outside world, who discuss their social lives,
offer to come round for half an hour before they go to a
party which is apparently happening near your house, make
comments you no longer understand such as 'I've been in
bed for three days with a cold', and conspicuously do not
say 'why don't I take the baby so that you can have some
time off?'

No matter how much I try to retain my self, my shape,
within the confines of this trial, it is like trying to resist the
sleep an anaesthetic forces upon a patient. I believe that my
will can keep me afloat, can save me from being submerged;
but consciousness itself is unseated, undermined, by the
process of reproduction. By having a baby I have created a
rival consciousness, one towards which my bond of duty is
such that it easily gains power over me and holds me in an
enfeebling tithe. My daughter quickly comes to replace me
as the primary object of my care. I become an undone task,
a phone call I can't seem to make, a bill I don't get around
to paying. My life has the seething atmosphere of an
untended garden. Strangely this neglect troubles me most
where it is most superficial: with the baby's birth a lifetime
of vanity vanished into thin air. Like gestures of love that
abruptly cease, I come to value my habit of self-adornment
only with its disappearance: it was proof that I cared, and
without it I feel a private sense of sad resignation, as if some

optimistic gloss has been stripped from my life. Sometimes I think back to that history of caring – as a self-conscious child, an anxious teenager, an attempted woman of fashion – amazed that it could have ended so precipitately, for it was in its modest way a civilisation, a city built from the days of my life. The last chapter of this history – pregnancy – was as vivid as any other: it contained no hint of an ending, no clue that things were about to change. It is as if some disaster has occurred which has wiped me out, an earth-quake, a falling meteor. When I look at old photographs of myself they seem to resemble the casts of Pompeii, little deaths frozen in time. I haunt the ruin of my body, a mournful, restless spirit, and I feel exposed, open to the air, the weather, and to the scrutiny of others. I know that there must be some physical future for me, but it is bogged down in planning problems, in administrative backlog. I hold out no great hopes for it in any case. The bright little body of my daughter takes up all my time. It is like a new house, a new project. I'll be lucky if I ever find the time to make the long journey back to myself, to the old ruin, and hurl a coat of paint over it before the winter of middle age sets in.

My daughter's pure and pearly being requires con-siderable maintenance. At first my relation to it is that of a kidney. I process its waste. Every three hours I pour milk into her mouth. It goes around a series of tubes and then comes out again. I dispose of it. Every twenty-four hours I immerse her in water and clean her. I change her clothes.

When she has been inside for a period of time I take her outside. When she has been outside for a period of time I bring her in. When she goes to sleep I put her down. When she awakes I pick her up. When she cries I walk around with her until she stops. I add and subtract clothes. I water her with love, worrying that I am giving her too much or too little. Caring for her is like being responsible for the weather, or for the grass growing: my privileged relation-ship with time has changed, and though these tasks are not yet arduous they already constitute a sort of serfdom, a slavery, in that I am not free to go. It is a humbling change. It represents, too, a reckoning of my former freedom, my distance from duty. The harness of motherhood chafes my skin, and yet occasionally I find a predictable integrity in it too, a freedom of a different sort: from complexity and choice and from the reams of unscripted time upon which I used to write my days, bearing the burden of their authorship. It does not escape me that in this last sentiment I am walking over the grave of my sex. The state of mother-hood speaks to my native fear of achievement. It is a demotion, a displacement, an opportunity to give up. I have the sense of history watching, from its club chair, my response to this demotion with some amusement. Will I give in, graciously, gratefully, handing back my life as some-thing I had on loan? Or will I put up a fight? Like moving back from the city to the small town where you were born, before exclaiming at its tedium you are advised to remember that other people live here, have always lived here. Men, when they visit, are constrained by no such considerations of tact. But it is not merely a taboo against complaint that makes the hardship of motherhood inadmissable: like all loves this one has a conflicted core, a grain of torment that buffs the pearl of pleasure; unlike other loves, this conflict has no possibility of resolution.

The baby's physical presence in my life is not unlike a traveller's custody of a very large rucksack. On the subway people tut and sigh at our double bulk, the administrative headache of us, and stream away at stations leaving us struggling with straps and overflowing detritus on the platform. We career into tables at restaurants, knock fragile things off shelves in shops, are clodhopping and clumsy and yet curiously invisible. Because I am the baby's home there is nowhere I can leave her, and soon I begin to look at those who walk around light and free and unencumbered as if they were members of a different species. When occasionally I do go out without her I feel exposed, like something that has lost its shell. The litany of the baby's requirements continues regardless of hour, season or location, and because her proclivities are not those of the adult world, when we are at large routine acquires the distinctive flavour of anarchy. She shrieks uncontrollably in quiet places, grows hungry where it is impossible for me to feed her, excretes where it is pristine: it is as if I myself have been returned to some primitive, shameful condition, being sick in expensive shops, crying on buses, while other people remain aloof and unpitying. My daughter emanates unprocessed human need where the world is at its most civilised; and while at first I am on the side of that world, which I have so recently left, and struggle to contain and suppress her, soon, like so many mothers, I come to see something inhuman in civilisation, something vain and deathly. I hate its precious, fragile trinkets, its greed, its lack of charity. Compassion worms its way into me: but whether it is just sentiment, an annexe of my love for my daughter, or a constitutional change I can't really say.

I become confined to one room, a development that represents a surrender, a battle lost. As my daughter becomes both more complex and more dangerous, my respect for her increases in proportion to others' disdain. The prospect of protecting her and the adult world from each other grows dark and unappealing. I can no longer face dragging her around after me. She is crawling now and has likes and dislikes. She has changed from rucksack to escaped zoo animal. Being in places that do not contain her requires me to be her tamer. Increasingly I remain at home with her, and as first stairs and then drawers and bookshelves and coffee tables acquire the potential for danger and riot, we become fenced in, cornered in the one safe space: the kitchen. My daughter zig-zags around it, maddened by confinement. It is winter and the garden is too wet and cold for her to crawl in. She beats on the door with her fists, desperate to escape. The floor is flooded to ankle height with her toys. Unidentifiable matter describes paths, like the trail of a snail, over walls and surfaces. The room has acquired a skin, a crust of dried milk upon which old food sits like a sort of eczema. The kitchen is pollinated with every substance with which my daughter comes into contact: mess spreads like a force of nature, unstoppable. My clothes are limed with it; I find gobbets in my hair, on my shoes. I wash and rinse and scrub but a strong undertow of entropy appears to govern this overheated little space and chaos is forever imminent, encroaching. Time hangs heavy on us and I find that I am waiting, waiting for her days to pass, trying to meet the bare qualification of life which is for her to have existed in time. In this lonely place I am indeed not free: the kitchen is a cell, a place of no possibility. I have given up my membership of the world I used to live in. Sometimes I listen to music or read, and it is like a ray of light coming in from outside, bright and painful, making me screw up my eyes. When we go for a walk I see young women in the street, beautiful and careless, and a pang of mourning for some oblique, lost self makes my heart clench. I look down at my daughter sleeping in her push-chair, the dark fringe of her lashes forming arcs on her pale skin, and a contrary wind of love gusts over me; and for some time this is how I am, blown this way and that, careering around like a crazy, febrile gauge trying to find north.

It is during this phase, when my relish for the job of motherhood approximates that of the average filing clerk, when love and grief have me in a tug-of-war and the world outside wears the strange glitter of the past, of the unreachable, that I read again Coleridge's poem 'Frost At Midnight'.

> The frost performs its secret ministry,
> Unhelped by any wind. The owlet's cry
> Came loud – and hark, again! loud as before.
> The inmates of my cottage, all at rest,
> Have left me to that solitude, which suits
> Abstruser musings: save that at my side
> My cradled infant slumbers peacefully.
> 'Tis calm indeed! so calm, that it disturbs
> And vexes meditation with its strange
> And extreme silentness. Sea, hill, and wood,
> This populous village! Sea, and hill, and wood,
> With all the numberless goings on of life,
> Inaudible as dreams!

This has always been one of my favourite poems, but reading it again I realise with a shock that like many childless people I had never noticed the baby. It is, admittedly, a well-behaved baby: even so, its presence causes me now to feel resentment and some awe. I am grudgingly amazed that Coleridge managed to write a poem at all with a baby in the room, let alone one that claims to find conditions over-quiet. I begin to see my predicament as the result of some deep failure of sensibility, some meanness of soul. I remember once, as a student, reading an advertisement in the paper for summer jobs in a fish factory on a remote ice-floe in Greenland. You were flown out there for three months, made to work sixteen-hour shifts, shuttled between barracks and factory by bus. There would be continuous daylight, nothing to do except work in the factory, and communication with the outside world would be extremely difficult. At the end of three months – stunned, mad, reeking of fish – you were dumped on the tarmac with your money and allowed to go home and get on with your life. My experience of motherhood is beginning to bear an alarming resemblance to this advertisement. I have been waiting, I realise, to come back, to return to thought and beauty and meaning, and when I read 'Frost at Midnight' it is slightly painful, as if blood were returning to a numbed limb.

It is a poem about sitting still, about the way children act as anchors on the body and eventually the mind. The father frets at this stillness as at the quiet of imprisonment: he is listening for the world, so hard that he can hear the frost being laid down outside. Presently he begins to fathom the depths of himself, to dive deeper into the moment he inhabits. He remembers himself as a child, at boarding school, his loneliness and the harshness of his teachers, the terrible hope he cherished that at any minute the door to the classroom would open and someone would come in, someone he loved. These memories arouse in him the profoundest feelings of love for his child, as if every separation he has endured in his life can be mended by this moment of their closeness.

> Dear Babe, that sleepest cradled by my side,
> Whose gentle breathings, heard in this deep calm,
> Fill up the interspersed vacancies
> And momentary pauses of the thought!
> My Babe so beautiful! it thrills my heart
> With tender gladness, thus to look at thee,
> And think that thou shalt learn far other lore
> And in far other scenes! For I was reared
> In the great city, pent 'mid cloisters dim,
> And saw naught lovely but the sky and stars.

This love is a restitution; it is like a new place, from which the old country, the unhappy past, can safely be viewed. For a writer such a love can represent the attainment of narrative authority over life itself. He imagines his baby grown up, wandering the world, seeing marvels. Confinement becomes freedom, ugliness beauty: parenthood is redemptive, transformative, creative. It is the means by which the self's limits are broken open and entrance found to a greater landscape. Coleridge does not mention nappies,

noise, bits of old food. I don't think this is just because it's
the night shift. His poem is written in the present tense: it
describes a moment, surrounded, by implication, by other
moments, by noise and disarray. Perhaps moments, now,
are all there is. But this is a moment to which he brings his
gift, which is language, a moment in which his love finds a
voice. In this moment he contains the world, its good and
its bad. In this moment he experiences an elemental
greatness.

> Therefore all seasons shall be sweet to thee,
> Whether the summer clothe the general earth
> With greenness, or the redbreast sit and sing
> Betwixt the tufts of snow on the bare branch
> Of mossy apple-tree, while the nigh thatch
> Smokes in the sun-thaw; whether the eavedrops fall,
> Heard only in the trances of the blast,
> Or if the secret ministry of frost
> Shall hang them up in silent icicles,
> Quietly shining to the quiet Moon.

Help

When summer came I started to feel stuck. My daughter was five months old and she was everywhere, like something sweet but sticky on my life, like molasses, like glue. It wasn't her fault: it was in her nature, so I read in books, to attach herself, as if I was a wall and she was the vine growing up it. What I wanted was to train her on to something else so that she could stay standing for periods while I briefly absented myself. In the stories I used to read as a child parents were remote, romantic figures who were frequently out or away on some mysterious business, or kept late hours, holding elegant parties downstairs while the children hung perilously over the banisters eavesdropping. These parents were often fated for tragic early deaths: their liner would sink or their automobile plunge, furs and cigarette holders flying, off a cliff in St Tropez, leaving the children apparently unaffected and free to pursue wonderful adventures. There was usually a nanny figure in the background of these stories, someone warm and comfortable who covered every inch of the house like a deep-pile carpet, later to be rolled up and kept in an upstairs room when she was old: a palliative for feelings of loneliness and abandonment, a magical solution to the problem of missing parents.

My own parents always cared for us themselves. Once they went away on holiday, leaving us with a woman who presented us at breakfast with whatever parts of our supper we had refused to eat the night before, but generally they operated a system of credit with a few other families. We would go to their houses, or they would come to ours. Now, those of my friends who had children seemed to labour under the stress of lean, contingent arrangements which added to rather than relieved their enslavement: racing out of the house to drop them at a childminder, racing back from work to collect them, frantically bargaining over minutes with au pairs or nannies; panicked negotiations conducted against the threat of some certain expiry, as if at six o'clock the nanny would vanish in a puff of smoke, or the childminder put the baby outside in the rain. There was no slack, no lubricant empty hours. It was precisely the luxury of those hours, those free and careless hinges between this event and that, that I secretly desired to purchase back, for with the birth of my daughter they had disappeared and were not expected to return for some years. Months after her birth I still found myself affronted and incredulous, as if at some foreign and despicable justice, by the fact that I could no longer sleep in or watch a film or spend a Saturday morning reading, that I couldn't stroll unfettered in the warmth of a summer's evening or go swimming or wander down to the pub for a drink. The loss of these things seemed a high, an exorbitant price to pay for the privilege of motherhood; and though much was given back to me in the form of my daughter it was not payment in kind nor even in a different coin, was not in fact recompense of any sort. My loss and my gain were unrelated, were calculated without the aim of some final, ultimate balance.

The deep-pile nanny, the nanny who exists to cushion the impact of parenthood, was, I discovered, the preserve of the wealthy. All other forms of childcare appeared to operate on the principles of a public callbox. You push coins into the slot. When your money runs out you are abruptly and unceremoniously cut off. Among people I knew, this rudimentary facsimile of freedom was used to cover the precise hours when the parents were at work. Babysitters were brought in to cover those futile stretches of time – evenings – when children are asleep and adults confined to the house. The times in between seemed to be your own affair. I knew of only one couple whose childcare arrangements extended to the weekend: they were rich and unsentimental.

My experiences with babysitters had, so far, been comical and sad. When my daughter was asleep, and hence unaware of the counterfeit I was manoeuvring into my place for those stolen hours, the babysitter would arrive. I would sit with her talking about my daughter, about what to do should she awake, about every aspect of her care. These precautions, like the safety demonstrations routinely given on airplanes, had a certain pointlessness: the occasion for their use would almost certainly not arise; if it did, a catastrophe would have occurred that was somewhat beyond their powers of rescue. Nevertheless, I enjoyed these conversations. Some loneliness was relieved by them, as if in the babysitter I had encountered a kindred spirit, someone who would, for a few hours, understand what it was to be me. Sometimes it seemed that I was enjoying the conversation so much that I did not intend to go out after all. 'She'll be fine,' the babysitter would say, over and over again until the phrase penetrated my consciousness sufficiently to inform me that I should leave. Having left, I would telephone, repeatedly. 'She's fine,' the babysitter would say. I would vow to call again in half an hour, to come home early. When I returned I would go and stare at her asleep in her baby carriage and her sleep would seem to me to be knowing and mysterious and slightly wounded, to be full of some experience in which I had not played a part, as if she had just come back from university or from a trip around the world.

Sometimes this encounter with a babysitter would remind me of the possibility of finding someone to care for my daughter for some of the time she spent awake.

Thinking of it, I would become suffused with feelings of relief and happiness, and with a sort of disbelief: first that such a possibility existed, and second that I had not made use of it, was not at this very moment making use of it. I would go instinctively to the telephone, as if a kindly person were waiting on the other end who would offer to send someone straight over, and stand there dumbly with the receiver in my hand. Who should I call? How should I begin my search? The person I had in mind was to be found not in the Yellow Pages but amidst choirs of heavenly angels, or in the pages of a storybook. She was wise, competent, kind, loving. Her salary was modest and vocational; her hours were love's own. She had no earthly existence, but sort of materialised on my doorstep each morning, took the baby reassuringly from my arms, wiped away my tears and said things like, *You just go off and enjoy yourself, we'll have a lovely time here, won't we?* She was the projection of my conflicted self; she resolved the fact that I never wanted to leave my daughter with the unfortunate truth that if I didn't I would never again be able to do anything else. The only way this truth could be made palatable was for its essence to be disguised. Handing over my child was to be not an act of dereliction but of gracious and logical concession, of glad surrender.

A friend of mine knew a woman called Rosa, who sometimes cleaned her house. Rosa came from Spain. She was saving up to emigrate to America, and wanted work. I asked my friend whether she thought Rosa might be able to look after my daughter. Cautiously, my friend replied that she thought she would not. She admitted that she had left her own children with her once or twice and had been disappointed. Tactfully she did not specify the reasons for her disappointment: I gained an impression of something vague and insubstantial, an impression my enthusiasm was easily able to overpower. Rosa was a small woman, tiny and nervous as a bird. She rode a bicycle around London, pedalling fast, she said, to keep commitments that stacked up each day in an unstable tower; for she had recently lost all her savings, a matter of some ten thousand pounds, to what appeared to be a sort of confidence man, a trickster who had offered to invest the money for her, and now she was driven to recoup it by taking on more work than she could really do in the time. She had grown up on a farm in northern Spain, she told me, running wild with her brothers and sisters. She had been happy in this innocent era: since then, she seemed to have found the world disappointing. She had lived in Switzerland for some years with a man. Now she lived with her sister, a hairdresser, in a council flat in south-east London.

I felt sorry for Rosa, and felt, too, that my own need intersected with hers: her need for money and my need for time were limitless and apparently perfectly matched. I agreed an arrangement of hours with her. The appointed day was rainy and dark. My daughter and I awaited Rosa, nervously, like people at an airport. An hour passed before the telephone rang. It was Rosa, who had been wandering around in the rain unable to find our house. I gave her directions. On the phone she had been apologetic, but when she arrived she was angry. She cursed the British weather. She cursed our house, which had been so difficult to find. She did not acknowledge my daughter, who lay in my arms with startled eyes; and a hard knot of unease lodged itself in my chest, a strong presentiment of trouble and of wrong. I offered Rosa tea and coffee, took her wet things, and yet behind these ministrations I suddenly knew that I was captive in my house, held hostage by a stranger whom I had to find some way of convincing to leave. My daughter began to cry. I sat down with her to give her a bottle of milk. Rosa asked me if she could look around the house and helplessly I agreed. She was gone a long time. I heard her upstairs, moving slowly around. A strange sort of terror came over me, so that my thoughts drifted far away and my mind lapsed into a blank sleep. This interlude was so preoccupying that when Rosa materialised again in the doorway the sight of her made me jump, as if I had forgotten she was in the house. It's nice, she said softly. I began to talk, gabbling nonsensically, asking her questions. She told me how she and her brothers and sisters used to spend their time killing bees that lived in a hive in their garden, squashing them with knives. She told me about her employers, their dirty homes, their disgusting habits. She asked me if I made a lot of money. My daughter had fallen into a deep, stunned sleep and so I put her in her crib. Rosa, I said shrilly, I'm afraid we've changed our plans. I told her we were moving house, leaving the country, had been called away suddenly. I offered to pay her for the whole day. I apologised, repeatedly. To my surprise she took the news without protest and was gone.

Having failed in one bid for escape, it was some time before I attempted another. Presently a friend suggested Celia, a Brazilian woman who was trying to get a teaching qualification in the afternoons and wanted work in the mornings. Celia came garlanded with encomiums. She had looked after my friend's children, with success. She was good with babies, and kind to older children. When she took them for walks she put slips of paper in their pockets with their address and telephone number written down, in case they got lost. I found this an unnerving precaution, but decided to take my friend's word for it. Celia was a large, gentle person with long black hair. She had come to England ten years earlier to be with her boyfriend, and when the relationship broke up she stayed. She desired, fervently, to better her circumstances; she dreamed of being a primary school teacher, a dream kept beyond her reach by her stubbornly and profoundly accented English, an accent that no amount of classes and courses could erase. Celia's discourse was full of the struggles of her existence: she was what people cruelly call a victim, of herself and others. Bad luck pursued her; pitfalls lay forever in her path. She suffered from headaches and depression, and from extreme reactions to bad weather and darkness. The menial nature of part-time work ground her down. One employer had made her vacuum stairs so incessantly that she had damaged her back. Another insisted that she spend hours ironing his collection of flamboyant shirts, standing over her as she went over the ruffles and cuffs, making her do them again. She had gone to work in a shop and been accused of stealing, threatened with the police. Some lack of assertiveness, some bleak tendency to acceptance, left her unable to convince others of her innocence. Celia came to my house on the understanding that her contract would be terminated at any minute by her hopes: that she would return to Brazil, that she would get a teaching job, that her computer course would bear some unspecified fruit. In the meantime, she laid my daughter on a rug on the kitchen floor and spoke to her in soft Portuguese, dangling a toy before her eyes like a hypnotist's pendant.

Upstairs, my reunion with freedom, so longed for, was panicked and unsatisfactory, and not only because my daughter exerted on me so strong a magnetism from her rug down below that I would emerge from my study every few minutes to sit on the stairs and listen for signs of distress. There was something brutal in our separation, an atmosphere I remembered from past instances of dark compulsion: the atmosphere of Sunday nights when I would return to my boarding school, of exams and injections and doctors' surgeries, of rejection and disfavour and punishment; of pain, too, more recently recalled, the adult pain of unhappiness and of things happening that you did not want to happen, but which happened nonetheless. It surprised and distressed me that all of my life that did not include my daughter or relate directly to her must now be lived in this hated, familiar dark; that its sum must be increased, its space extended like catacombs dug beneath my happiness, when I had vowed to shut the door on it for ever. I would go down to the kitchen on some pretext or other and my daughter would sometimes cry when she saw me, her eyes confused and imploring; and I would feel beset by my power to end our mutual misery. My failure to do so plagued me, given that I mostly spent my expensive hours alone worrying about what was going on downstairs.

Celia failed her English exam and entered dark times. She began to come very late or not at all, telephoning with stories of headaches and missed buses. I had taken on some work, and during one of Celia's last-minute absences was driven to sit frantically typing at my computer with a deadline some forty-five minutes away while my daughter lay crying on my study floor. When Celia did come she was silent and morose, walking as if every step hurt her, her eyes shining with unhappiness. She admitted that the man she was involved with was treating her badly. My daughter, too, had seen through our little ruse. In Celia's sad face she read the warning of her imminent abandonment, and she struggled to prevent it. From upstairs I could hear the siren of her cry, and occasionally caught a strained, desperate note in Celia's musical utterances, heard the frantic squeaking of the baby carriage's hinges as she tried too hard to lull my daughter into sleep. One day she told me that she was starting a new course and would only be able to come for two hours a week. We agreed that I would have to look for someone else.

Flicking idly through television channels one evening, I found myself plunged into the middle of a documentary about the travails of rich American housewives. A woman with a sharp tanned face and expensive-looking hair was sitting on a leather sofa discussing the deficiencies of her children's nanny. The nanny was glimpsed in the background, a blur of dark skin, her head ducked, putting toys in a box. She was Peruvian, it transpired, and had left four children of her own behind in order to come to America and make sufficient money to support them. She saw them once or twice a year. You know, said the woman, Maria is *wonderful* with my kids, but sometimes I get the feeling that she's, you know, kind of *too* wonderful. I mean, I *know* that she probably misses her kids, and I *know* that you can't, like, *forbid* her to touch my kids, but at the end of the day, they're not her kids, you know? Like, the other day I was in the pool and Maria was in the hot tub with my daughter, and she had my daughter on her lap, and I'm like, you know, *put her down, she knows how to sit in the hot tub*! She tossed her immaculate hair with pique.

I put an advertisement in the local paper, and was surprised when a man rang up in response. His name was Stefan. He was Slovenian. He was twenty, and had worked in London as an au pair for a year. Now he was doing a PhD at university, but needed a part-time job. I invited him to the house for a talk. He was slight and dapper, with the attire and demeanour of an accountant. He carried a briefcase and his English was aristocratic, shot through with glassy slivers of Eastern Europe. I offered him a glass of wine and a cigarette, both of which he accepted, and we sat in the garden. He had enjoyed his experiences as an au pair. He liked cooking and housekeeping. He had loved the family he worked for: their children, he told me, were adorable. He still saw the parents, indeed they were coming round that very evening for dinner. He produced a reference from them: it was glowing. Their youngest child had been four months old when Stefan had joined the family. She was very special, said Stefan, very intelligent. He shook his head, smiling, as if her charms were impossible to convey. I asked him about his PhD. It appeared that he was studying transport links to London's airports. My daughter remained firmly seated in my lap during this time. Stefan's manner towards her was polite but understated, as if they were business colleagues. She betrayed no feelings about the matter either way. We agreed that he would start the next week.

The telephone rang and rang in the following days, and each time I would pick it up and hear the voices of women, voices old and young, voices bespeaking hardship or hope or desperation, or a sort of blithe confusion, as if they didn't know whether it was for a job or a second-hand ironing board that they were calling, and didn't much care. We've already found somebody, I said, over and over again; I'm sorry. These negotiations were shabby, frank, guilty, devoid of love or care. There was a harshness, the harshness of money and survival, just beneath their surface. It seemed incredible to me that I was bartering with my daughter's small existence in this way; that by coming into the world she had created a problem which I was solving so randomly and with such fearful incompetence. Stefan arrived punctually and began doing the ironing. He asked if he could do the shopping later, and what we would like for supper. Did we like cabbage? He had a sheaf of Slovenian recipes up his sleeve. While we were talking the telephone rang, and I handed him my daughter. His face was alarmed. He held her as one might hold a small bomb. When I put down the telephone he handed her back. I saw that immediate action was necessary. I stood about for a while and then said I had to go and do some work. I placed my daughter on the sofa two feet away from where Stefan stood, iron in hand, and left the room. Eavesdropping from the stairs, I counted a long moment of silence. Presently, I heard a sort of clucking sound, such as one might make to goad along a horse. My daughter began to grumble, and the clucking got louder. Before long, she began to cry. Don't cry, I heard Stefan say brightly, don't cry, baby. I went back downstairs. My daughter lay where I had left her on the sofa, screaming, with Stefan doing a sort of dance of comfort above her, as if she were emanating some powerful heat that prevented him from getting too close. You've got to pick her up, I explained. I felt profoundly tired.

Stefan's efficiency quickly gathered to itself a range of housekeeping measures: he polished furniture, dusted, stocked the larder. He had the air of a butler in a stately home, attentive and discreet. The kitchen hung with the boiled-clothes smell of cabbage. Occasionally he would take my daughter for a walk in her stroller and, obeying my orders to return if she cried, quickly came back again. She was given back to me, entire, like something too big to be sent, like something impossible. I gained the distinct impression of her inferiority to his former, beloved charge. I told Stefan that I was very sorry, but that we had to have somebody who could look after the baby. He accepted his dismissal with some charm. The next day he came back again and rang on the doorbell. His flatmates, he told me, had convinced him that his sacking was unfair and merited compensation. Drily, I asked what sort of compensation he had in mind. A month's salary, he replied, was the norm. I offered him a week's. He accepted and went away, having obviously found the conversation difficult.

All through these weeks I retained an impression of my daughter's eyes, dark and bright and locked on mine as she was passed from one stranger, with their story, their particular body and breath, their indefinable aura, to another. I saw in her eyes bewilderment and acceptance and some evidence of bravery, as she viewed me across the gulf of my life, the gulf I had put between us. She had tried, in some small way, to make it work. I understood that she would have taken whatever I had offered, had I forced her to, but I had never given it time, nor the ultimate sacrifice of my own sincere assurance that it would work out. I had discovered, too, that those hours I had purchased back were damaged and second-hand. They were cramped and unsatisfactory; they were hours whose crazy ticking could be heard. Living those hours was like living in a taxi cab. Working in them was hard enough; pleasure, or at least rest, was unthinkable. I couldn't fit my world into a space carved, as it seemed to me, from my daughter's own flesh. Besides, I had conveyed to her distinctly the fact that I thought her abandonment was unreasonable, her protests fair: I wasn't ready, it seemed, to let her love somebody else.

Late one night, the telephone rang. It was Rosa. She was ringing to let us know how badly we had treated her. You people, she said, you pay slave wages. You are rich and you pay slave wages for slave labour. You are disgusting. Your house is disgusting. She demanded money in recompense. She had seen a large cheque on my desk during her tour of the house. What had I done to deserve that money? It was she who slaved all day. Her tirade became obscene, hysterical. She swore, she impugned. I held the receiver away from my ear and looked out through the dark glass over London and into the night. When I listened again, Rosa was still talking. You are a horrible woman, she said. She put down the phone.

Don't Forget to Scream

We moved out of the city to a university town, a place where people lived in order to forget that the rest of the world existed. There was little crime here, or chaos, or traffic, or noise, or dirt, or difference. It was all held at bay, as if by a magic circle, by the ring road, beyond which lay a tundra of the unwanted, of petrol stations and roundabouts, of factories and straggling conurbations and red, scarred swathes of land where new housing was going up. The ring road pulsed night and day with cars and trucks that circled the ancient buildings and cobbled streets like predators. Wherever you were you could hear its submerged roar, like that of the sea.

Our house was in a residential area that had the texture of a suburb or prairie. It was here that the grand terraces of the town centre began to separate themselves, if only by a few feet, into houses whose cramped architecture fancifully suggested ranches and châteaux. The streets bristled with the frontiers of fences and garden gates. Our road was an artery by which the local shops could be reached, and saw discreet but considerable traffic. Sturdy women in their fifties wearing thick sandals and flowered dresses ploughed up and down it on bicycles. Bearded men with broad, womanish hips dressed all in beige plodded past our window, walking small, yappy dogs. The men were mute and miserable and cringed from encounter; but the women swept down our road like storms, cyclones of disapproval, the wind of their censure whistling through cracks in doors and windows as they passed. They briskly eyed our over-grown front lawn, the crates of empty wine bottles outside our door. Such women had no fear of ridicule or rebuke as they pedalled on in their summer dresses, baskets creaking, showing the white, freckled slabs of their arms, remon-strating with the occasional motorist or dog-owner or litter-bug. They ruled this peculiar enclave, with its capacious, obedient streets, and their spirit presided over what life presumed to struggle through its oppressive, middle-aged soil.

The other mothers I saw all seemed to be far older than I. In London I had rarely encountered people out with children, but here the high street teemed with them. Our strollers bowed and whirled and sidestepped in a pavement minuet. I would occasionally find myself staring like a prude at women with grey hair and pregnant bellies, at grandmother-mothers with shoals of small children. Indeed, I had never seen so many children before in my life;

and yet sex was nowhere in the air, for the fathers of these children were hardly seen. The restaurants and cafés were filled with women; the shops and parks were filled with women. Early on a Sunday morning men could occasionally be sighted, pushing prams uncomfortably around the empty streets; but by lunchtime they had vanished again. The whole place had the atmosphere of a war, or a laboratory experiment, or the past. The women on bicycles who policed its sexless avenues themselves possessed a peculiar and disturbing girlishness, with their dumpy flowered dresses and thick white arms: the girlishness of nuns, of ageing virgins, of unmarried daughters. Their spiritual mothers were wiry, veined, white-haired women in court shoes and navy pleated skirts, with faces sharp as birds', who congregated outside the bank or the grocer's and conducted the pitiless business of their conversation.

I believed that I would never have lived in such a place when my life was my own; and although it is in the purpose of such places to ensure that it is not, to remove your life from your control and hence prevent it from becoming a public danger, I had to claim my share of responsibility in the matter of relinquishing London and the existence to which over the years my unfettered desire had given shape. I could not tell you how great this share was: I never had time or opportunity to quantify it. All I know is that it began to grow in me after I had a child: a second gestation, of dissatisfaction, sometimes of actual distress. A feeling of dispossession and rootlessness took hold of me, thrived in me, putative but vigorous, and it was only once I had ceased to house it and actually brought it to life that I saw it was merely a phantom, a construction. I had given, it seemed, concrete expression to my grief at the fact that I could no longer live the life that I had been living. I had moved away because I thought I no longer belonged where I was.

No sooner had I done it than I found myself remarkably restored. Everything that motherhood had seemed to put at an unbreachable remove now was obstructed by mere geography. The loneliness of hours spent with a baby at home merged with that of moving to a new, friendless and uncongenial place. What was staid and humdrum and restricting and depriving about motherhood found its incarnation in our surroundings. My life shed its burden, passed it on. Imagine, I found myself saying to my partner one day, how much easier it would be looking after children if you weren't stuck in this boring hole, if you had all your friends around and places to go in the evening and things to do at the weekend. You mean in London, he said.

So our life in the provinces quickly took on the tenor of a prison sentence, whose term could not be set because of the difficulty of admitting to ourselves or others that we had erred. There was an etiquette, I felt, to the making of such mistakes: they ought to take time, although we did have a friend who had moved out of London and back in the space of a few days. He played in a tennis four on Saturdays, and managed to relocate his family to the north of England, realise his error, and bring them all back again without missing a game. In any case, at first our new life felt, if not exactly right, then at least like something more bearable than a mistake. It was late summer, and in a languorous heatwave we swam daily in a nearby river, a wide, still ribbon of water that meandered through a great meadow where cows and wild horses grazed. People boated on this river: elderly couples in motor launches, boisterous groups on canal-boat holidays, people sailing dinghies down this quaint, pastoral strait as if it were the sea. There were men dressed in sailing garb – jaunty caps and handkerchiefs tied around the neck – that would have looked more at home in a San Francisco nightclub. There were couples you could glimpse through the fishbowls of their glazed, airtight cabins, the man sitting grimly at the wheel, the woman flicking about the cabin with a duster or making cups of unearned tea. On another stretch of river people poled punts through the thick green waters; students and tourists mostly, their loud laughter or silence alike indicative of self-consciousness, for this was a well-worn idyll, an enactment of privilege derived from the pages of *Brideshead Revisited.* Once I saw a group of students on a punt, the boys dressed in white flannels and boaters, the girls in diaphanous dresses and straw hats. Someone even carried a teddy bear. They had a picnic basket and an old-fashioned gramaphone on board, from which emanted loud, distorted strains of Edith

Piaf. They held champagne glasses. One boy waved the bottle at other punts as they passed. They were a strange group, ill-fitted for the hedonism at which they strained: the boys were spotty and beak-nosed, the girls dumpy and bespectacled. Their riotousness was uncertain, bordering clumsily on abuse. I cringed for them, but the taint of their pretentious outing remained on my mind over the long months, like a warning, impossible to rub away.

Slowly the year rolled over: summer turned to autumn. My daughter learned to crawl and then to stand as the days drew in and it started to rain. Her development was not, as I had expected, taking the joyful form of a sprightly liberation from the paralysis of babyhood. Instead it was a slow and frustrating business. Watching her was like watching a film running backwards. Her body was tormented by some invisible force that made her get up and fall over again and again, that caused her to struggle and stretch, like someone drowning, for a chair leg or table top to which to cling. It was as if she were fighting to emerge from quicksand. My head ached with the tension of her efforts. It became dangerous to leave her unguarded for even a minute, for her physical drive was like sand issuing from a fathomless hourglass, like time: it flowed from her in a constant stream which we fought to channel and contain, spilling hazardously over when the telephone or a knock at the door occasioned a moment of neglect. I recalled remarks I had carelessly heard other parents use, phrases like *she never stops* or *she's on the go all the time*, and pondered what they actually meant. An instant's distraction would find my daughter inching over the top of the stairs, pulling electrical leads that were about to bring the kettle or iron down on top of her, delving into the rubbish. She husked records from their sleeves and shredded letters in their envelopes with the speed of a harvesting peasant. She aimed herself at bottles of bleach or hot cups of tea, trundling across rooms like a slow but deadly missile and changing course only if someone actually went and stood between her and her target. Suddenly our life was like a drama in which a bomb is being disabled against the clock. We were, all at once, the slaves of time, and we kept our daughter to the kitchen so as better to contain her ticking, to contain her power to destroy. Only when she was upended, neutralised by sleep, did the ticking stop; interludes which washed swiftly and soundlessly past us like flood waters, bearing away the pleasure of books or conversation too quickly for us to do more than grab at them.

The business of looking after a child possesses a core of unruliness, a quality of continual crisis, and my version of motherhood lacked, I saw, the aspect of military organisa-tion with which such a core should be approached. I do not use the word 'military' lightly: conscription to the world of orthodox parenthood demands all the self-abnegation, the surrender to conformity, the relish for the institutional, that the term implies. People understood this in the town in which we now lived. Its residential recesses were 'geared' to the good mother. This, I came to understand, was why so many mothers lived here. Here you could be free from the torments and temptations of life on the outside, from bars and movie theaters and shops selling impractical shoes. Here the restaurants had high chairs and changing facilities, the buses wide doors and recesses for prams. The exalted sphere of the university, its silence, its privileged, patriarchal enclaves, lived on undisturbed. A hierarchy was in place and its provision extended from the lowest to the highest.

A health visitor came to see us in our embattled kitchen. She produced sheaves of leaflets and laid each one lovingly on the table for me to study while behind her the baby looted her handbag undetected. Have you taken her to toddler group, the health visitor enquired. I had not. Like vaccinations and mother and baby clinics, the notion instilled in me a deep administrative terror. I took the baby to shops where I tried on clothes, to cafés in the centre where students sat packed in a fog of cigarette smoke. I took her for walks across bumpy fields where the stroller became mired in mud. I took her to London, where she cried frantically in noisy restaurants, in traffic jams. The health visitor produced a typed list of groups in my area. It helps, she said, to meet other mothers. You can chat, and even have a coffee if you feel like it. I sensed that I should feel abjectly grateful for this lowly provision. As it was I drank cup after cup of strong coffee alone, and smoked cigarettes in the garden when my daughter was asleep. I'll see, I said. I suppose it would be good for her to meet other babies. As far as I knew, my daughter believed that she was the only one of her kind. I worried that the truth might come as something of a shock.

The kitchen floor had a hard, tiled surface. We put down rugs, but in spite of them several times each day my daughter's head would make contact with it. She would pull herself to her feet and stand, often for ten or fifteen minutes, before falling slowly backwards, ramrod straight like a felled tree. During the long seconds of this fall, whoever was with her would run towards her, occasionally diving or skidding like a baseball player lunging for base or even fielding a cushion towards the spot upon which her head was about to make contact; and in the moment of impact they would freeze, suspended in a posture of horror and protest by the sound of her skull hitting the tiles. The narrative of her adventures ran on in the background of our lives like a radio. Sometimes we attended to them and sometimes we didn't, but some miniature quest was always underway, stairs being scaled, cupboards excavated, objects scientifically analysed for their properties. Pain had lent her a certain toughness, a core of bravado which made her unwilling to admit failure or distress. I would occasionally look up, alerted by silence, to find her hanging grimly from a cupboard door or from the rungs of a chair in which her feet had become trapped. The world of things was her unresting opponent, her wilderness, and she took the risk of its instability, its unpredictability. One day she pulled herself to her feet on the rungs of her heavy wooden highchair, and it fell on top of her. I watched from the doorway, too far away to intervene, as she fell straight back on to the tiles with the tower of the highchair bearing down on her. Her head hit the tiles with a crack. Seconds later, the highchair's protruding wooden tray smacked against her forehead with the force of a sledgehammer. I picked her up and ran out into the street with her. I didn't know what else to do. It was as if I were surrendering her, or making some appeal for her safety to the outside world. There was a dent in the centre of her forehead. It turned yellow with bruising. Every time I looked at it I felt ashamed.

One morning I found the health visitor's list under the kitchen table. It informed me that a toddler group was convening in fifteen minutes' time at a church hall a few streets away. We put on our coats and set out along the windy pavement beneath a low grey sky, hurrying through the indeterminate heart of a suburban mid-week morning, through the flat terrain of the unimportant, the un-occupied, for all the world as if we were rushing to make a train or a meeting or a thrilling date. The hall was a modern one-storey building attached to the flank of a Gothic church. Inside, a circle of empty chairs had been methodically placed around a tidy miniature landscape of toys. We were the first to arrive. A busy, nervous woman wearing a small silver crucifix on a chain around her neck told us to write our names on stickers and attach them to our clothes. We stood about, shy and agonised like people at a party. The woman asked me if this was my first time at the group and I said that it was. My daughter set off determinedly for the toys, displacing one of the chairs. She picked up a plastic fireman's helmet and put it on her head. I don't know if they'll all come, confided the woman anxiously. I shouldn't think they will. You see, the holidays have started. I asked which holidays these were. She mentioned the name of the expensive private school whose manicured playing fields bordered our garden. I wondered what these holidays had to do with me, and realised that the answer was nothing. So you see, said the woman, it might not be so good this week. Oh well, I said. Presently she asked me if I had lived here long. Only a few weeks, I replied. And is your husband attached to the university? she enquired.

Other women were arriving. I saw them through the windows, coming up the path with their strollers. Hel-lo, yodelled the organiser, beaming, hel-*lo*. She rushed hither and thither, administering stickers. My daughter's face was sombre beneath her helmet, her demeanour important. She tended the toys authoritatively. Presently she caught sight of me sitting alone and came over to place a plastic turtle with wheels and mad revolving eyes comfortingly in my lap. Released from their strollers, the other children moved towards the toy area like people arriving at work and began to occupy themselves. A small boy approached my daughter and stood silently in front of her until she relinquished the blue teddy bear in her hand. She appeared to understand perfectly what was going on, which was more than could be said for me. I had not conversed with anyone outside my family for several weeks, and now appeared to be suffering from a form of Tourette's syndrome. A woman asked me how I liked the area in which we were living, and to my concern I found myself embarked on a lengthy denunciation of it which I was apparently unable to curtail. I saw, as if from a great distance, her worried face, her uncomprehending eyes. So what do you do? I said abruptly. This only appeared to make the situation worse. Julia bakes *marvellous* cakes, the woman next to her informed me after a pause. Really? I said, with frantic delight. I've always thought I'd love to be a baker. Do you make any money out of it? The two women looked at each other like schoolgirls, with horrified eyes. What does your husband do? somebody asked me. When next I looked at my daughter, I saw that a child with straggling hair and crossed eyes was gripping her by her thick red curls and banging her head repeatedly on the floor. Cordelia! trilled the child's mother distractedly. Cordelia! The organiser was bringing out cups and saucers which clattered loudly in her shaking hands. Steam rose from a boiling kettle. She went about the room, bending discreetly towards the groups of talking women. *Coffee,* she mouthed to each one in a stage whisper, as if she were interrupting important meetings. Nearby, Cordelia's mother was discussing Cordelia's proclivities. Whenever she sees a black person, she said fondly, she just bursts into tears! It's quite embarrassing really, she added above the laughter of the others. She's obviously, you know, *a bit frightened.* They nodded their heads sympathetically, hands over their smiling mouths. *Coffee?* whispered the organiser next to my ear.

Over at the coffee station, a broad woman with a vast bosom and a brutal helmet of grey hair asked me how many children I had. One, I said. She appeared disappointed at this meagre reply. Oh well, she said, I'm sure there'll be more. Immediately I recognised her as one of a local species I had seen and heard countless times in the past weeks, at the doctor's surgery, at the shops. Before we came to live here, when we were looking for a house, we had met just such a woman whose mouldering property we had come to view. When we rang the doorbell she had burst forth, dressed like a plain-clothed nun, looking wildly around her. Where are they? she had cried. Who? we asked, bewildered. *The children!* she said. *Where are all the children?* I've got five, the woman before me now stated matter of factly. You'll find it gets easier. She told me that her eight-year-old daughter was about to go to France on an exchange programme. Gosh, that's quite young to be going away on your own, I said. How long is she going for? A year, said the woman breezily. So that's one less to worry about. She looked at me concernedly. That's what I mean when I say *it does get easier.* I saw that my daughter was standing on her own in the middle of the room. She looked bewildered. The organiser tinkled her spoon against her coffee cup. Ladies! she cried. Ladies! I think it's time for some songs, don't you? For the first time, I noticed that there was a man in the room. He wore thick glasses and his hair stood wildly on end, as if he were being electrocuted. He was sitting on his own. A small, plump girl clung silently to his knee.

We all sat on the chairs, in a circle with our children in our laps. The organiser placed herself at the centre. She was holding a teddy bear, not, as I had at first thought, as a child-substitute but as a girl-guidish symbol of leadership. Singing seemed rather an intimate thing to do with people I hardly knew, but it was, at least, preferable to conversation. We began with 'The Wheels on the Bus', a hymn to public transport to which everyone except me knew both the words and the accompanying hand movements. 'Twinkle, Twinkle, Little Star' followed. I was quite happy to sing, finding something profound and absolving in the naïvity of the words. I clutched my daughter's warm little body. Sometimes, in such moments, she and the world forgot their quarrel and convened to assure me that I could protect her, enclose her, look after her. She struggled in my arms and I set her down. She lurched intently across the floor and prised the teddy from the organiser's hands. I looked about for the man and saw that he had gone. Row, row? said the organiser to the group. There was a chorus of approval. I knew the tune of this one, but the words, I soon found, had changed.

Row, row, row your boat
Gently down the stream.
If you see a crocodile
Don't forget to scream!

The final line was followed by a communal shriek, pitched unthreateningly high so as not to frighten the children. Not long after, we left the town and moved elsewhere. The memory of our time there faded quickly, leaving the strange taste of a dream. Although she never learned the song, my daughter loved the scream that accompanied it. Even if the fluting sound she made was incongruously welcoming, I admired her ability to seize the punchline, the kernel of a thing. Every time you sang the words delight would dawn across her face, and she would remember, and scream.

A Valediction
to Sleep

My daughter's birthday chimes another anniversary besides hers: it has been a year since I had an uninterrupted night's sleep. I ponder this fact like someone who has been kept in exile by the machinations of some impenetrable bureaucracy, promised again and again that tomorrow or next week the passport, the tickets, the papers will come and they can return home; because for each night of that year I have sincerely believed that sleep will be returned to me. My hopes are tarnished, threadbare. I thirst for the privacy and solitude, for the oxygen of day's lung, night. Instead the hours of darkness are a bleak corollary of those of light, an unpeopled continuum in which I remain on duty, like a guard in a building from which everyone has gone home.

This can't, I am sure, be normal. I suspect some failure in myself: of force, of identity, of purpose. I remember hearing, in my pre-maternal days, of the phenomenon of 'broken nights', and remember too feeling the youth and vigour of my will flex itself at the mention of this and other examples of infant tyranny. If I ever have a child, I said – I hope only – to myself, *I simply won't let that happen.* A strange desire to crush the privileges, to deny the claims of children would beset me when I heard about the ways in which they ruled their parents; and I see it occasionally now, in other people, when I tell the story of my nights; their primitive desire for my harshness, for me to break the hold and hence the hopes, the optimism, the clamouring innocence of the very young. Perhaps children expect what we ourselves no longer dare to; or perhaps we feel sure in some deep and unprovable way that our own long and lonely nights were never so lovingly attended; that we were left, as the literature of the time advised, to cry.

I remember the night sleep left me. It happened in hospital. I had suspected nothing. Several hours earlier I had had a baby; people had come and gone, flowers had been brought. Darkness fell. Presently it was half past ten or so, time to go to sleep. I wrapped the baby up in blankets like a new purchase, a present that I would unwrap and look at again in the morning. I slept. When I woke again some time later, it was to realise with real surprise that the terrible, persistent wailing racketing through the ward was 'me', as people now say of their mobile phones. My new purchase had gone off in the dead of night like some alarm I didn't know how to disconnect. The penumbral bodies of the other women began to roll in their beds, like tethered boats in a sleeping harbour stirred by waves of noise.

Presently someone tutted. In the same ward the night before, under similar circumstances, I too had tutted. I wasn't tutting now. I felt for the first time the discomfiting spotlight of responsibility, its glare rude in the darkness, and since then I have not closed my eyes without the expectation of opening them again to that light which is not the blessed light of day but is rather a visitation, a spectre, a summons to the secret, lawless world of night. Sleep, like a great bear, a soft, warm, vigilant guardian of unconsciousness, had rolled away with a yawn and padded off elsewhere, never, it seems, to return. I have put bears in my daughter's crib, amongst other things, as if to suggest that I know something she doesn't about comfort and safety and sleep, but their glassy, affectless eyes are blind to our nightly dramas. Without the consecration of sleep, darkness is re-armed with all its mythical terror. I can't pretend that I don't feel it too, that by now I would be amazed if she *did* sleep through these sinister gulfs between the days, my childish fear of which has been re-ignited by hers. Repose has left our house, and I don't know how or from where to summon it back.

In the early months of my daughter's life I felt my own tiredness as a physical shock. The spring of activity, given no chance by night to uncoil, felt as if it were being wound tighter and tighter in my chest, derailing all my natural tensions and corralling them into one, great, explosive point of fatigue. In the morning I would sit up in bed, the room listing drunkenly about me, and would put a hand to my face, checking for some evidence of disfigurement: an eyebrow, perhaps, slipped down to my cheek, a deranged ear cluttering my forehead, a seam at the back of my skull gaping open. The day was sometimes a sticky mire to be laboriously crossed, the air unbreathable glue; and sometimes a frantic, untethered cloud speeding across the sky, upon which I could never gain a foothold. Once or twice the baby slept for a stretch of five or six hours, and I would wake feeling as if I had been punched. I began to speak with a curious lisp, and would put a hand to my mouth several times a day to check that my tongue was not lolling out of it.

Gradually the distinction between day and night dissolved entirely, and I became prey to daydreams and hallucinations, remembering conversations that had not occurred, glimpsing strange creatures through windows and in corners, a continual buzz of activity in my head both infernal and remote, as if a television had been left on in a next-door room. At night I began to experience a particularly sinister visitation: a second baby came to inhabit my dreams, one for whom my ministrations were so exacting that I could not attend to the first. This second baby would cry and I would feed it, informing the world thickly through the darkness when the first baby too started to cry that I could not feed that one as I was busy with this. I would wake with a start, convinced that I had rolled over and smothered it, or sweep the floor beside my bed with a frenzied hand, sure that it had fallen out, while the real baby slept on in her cradle.

As more time passed this elaborate spectre faded, and the muddled nights began to attain an insomniac clarity. My insides grew gritty, my nerves sharp. The baby continued to wake three or four times each night, and each time I was ready for her, trained and vigilant as a soldier. I no longer, it seemed, slept at all in the intervals, but merely rested silently like some legendary figure, itinerant, doughty and far from home. The reservoir of sleep I had accumulated through my life had run dry. I was living off air and adrenalin. Mercury ran through my veins. I wondered if this parched and dogged wraithe long since severed from its human past was in fact that dark stranger who walks the world of childhood wreathed in mystery: a parent.

The lesson of sleep is a lesson in loneliness. In Charlotte Bronte's *Jane Eyre,* the child Jane's cruel Aunt Reed locks her in the Red Room for the night with just such a lesson in mind, keen to instruct her in her orphaned state, to remind her not to presume that she is loved. Left without a candle in the ghostly chamber, Jane learns quickly enough that she is not; but her terror soon exceeds this sorry fact. Alone in the dark, she begins to dwell upon death. She suspects that her Uncle Reed died in that very room. In a frenzy of terror, she has a hallucinatory, or actual, encounter with a ghost.

She begins to scream and cry and beat at the door to be let out, and eventually the servants come.

'She has screamed out on purpose,' declared Abbot, in some disgust. 'And what a scream! If she had been in great pain one would have excused it, but she only wanted to bring us all here; I know her naughty tricks.'

Aunt Reed demands that Jane is returned to the room and locked in.

'I abhor artifice,' she says, 'particularly in children; it is my duty to show you that tricks will not answer; you will now stay here an hour longer, and it is only on condition of perfect submission and stillness that I shall liberate you then.'

Jane faints with fear; when she is finally retrieved, she is delerious and violently ill.

Much later, when Jane returns to attend Aunt Reed's deathbed, this experience is still in her mind. In the intervening years she has learned to understand night as the place in which truth is revealed; as the opposite to day, the dissimulator. Night is when young girls die of starvation and neglect in boarding schools; it is when mad secret wives prowl the corridors; it is when the homeless and friendless plead in vain for human clemency. Jane has reckoned with the night, and emerged formidable.

'I felt a determination to subdue her,' she says of her dying aunt, as she sits at her bedside one night, 'to be her mistress in spite both of her nature and her will.' Aunt Reed begins to ramble. She asks whatever happened to Jane Eyre.

'What did they do with her at Lowood? The fever broke out there, and many of the pupils died. She, however, did not die: but I said she did – I wish she had died!'

'A strange wish, Mrs Reed; why do you hate her so?'

Aunt Reed replies that it was jealousy. Her late husband loved the orphaned baby Jane, in spite of the fact that 'it would wail in its cradle all night long – not screaming heartily like any other child, but whimpering and moaning.' He made her promise, when he died, to look after the child, a promise she broke. Jane mightily confers her forgiveness on her aunt, but the woman hates her too much to accept it. She dies later that night. The next morning Jane and Aunt Reed's daughter Eliza come to pay their respects to the body. 'Neither of us,' Jane observes as they leave, 'had dropped a tear.'

I wonder whether I am constructing a fortress against notions of helplessness and abandonment. These notions are entertained, as they are refuted, by myself alone. At night I am plagued by the fact of my child's physical separateness from me, a fact I am at one minute tempted to conceal, the next to promulgate. My uncertainty about our mutual distinctness breeds in this division between day and night. I wonder whether my daughter has noticed that in one half of her life she is fed, admired, served, delighted in, played with and lavished with care, while in the other she is left on her own in the dark. By day her cries are met with brisk, even anxious service. By night, even if she manages to make a noise that sounds exactly like she has pushed her head through the bars of her cot and is being slowly strangled, they are increasingly ignored.

The secret life of parents, like that of lovers, is nocturnal and effervescent, full of strange pacts and compromises, of fallings-out and reconciliations both violent and meaningless. The search for the limits of love, it rapidly becomes clear, is indistinguishable from the search for the limits of our isolation. In this sense the night lies before the fact of being alone like a swathe of green-belt before the developer's eye, its pristine emptiness an invitation to fill, to despoil. The child quickly comes to question the orthodoxy of darkness, to express affront at the idea that emotion should be confined to the hours of daylight. I try to remember when and how I myself came to accept this convention, and suspect that it was very recently, perhaps only when it fell to me to pass it on, amidst so many other slightly unauthentic representations of the world, to my daughter. Restless nights stretch back through my recollection like an eerie avenue populated by myself alone: nights when I was afraid and dared not disturb my parents, and later, when I was unhappy and dared not disturb the cause of my unhappiness; or dared, and discovered that the end of love is the refusal to let the loved one sleep. It is also a method used in torture camps, as new parents will eagerly be told, usually by other parents; a piece of apocrypha frequently recounted in the manner of an SOS, an urgent call for rescue from a domestic torture camp to whose existence the free world displays a profound indifference. I want my daughter to find out how people cool and turn away when you won't let them alone, how assurance is destroyed where it is most desperately sought; and yet at the same time I want to recast this awful truth for her, to make it untrue. Sometimes the power I have to love her seems like the power to transform wrong into right, to turn night into day.

I meet a woman who tells me that her children, now grown up and gone away, never slept at night. She and her husband would take it in turns to get up with them, night after night, and take them downstairs to play until they were tired enough to go back to bed. They still don't really sleep, she says. Her son stays up late listening to music, the sole tenant now of those lonely hours. I suddenly see that sleep is something you have to learn, like table manners.

Conveniently, there are books on the subject. Many of them are written by doctors and therapists and hence are full of case histories, which I enjoy voyeuristically: a woman who would sit by her child's crib for hours beating a drum; a toddler who consumed a full bottle of milk every two hours, bottles which her parents would line up on the windowsill at the beginning of the night and then go in automatically at the stated intervals to hand to her; a child who could only go to sleep while his parents were sitting on the sofa downstairs watching television, an activity they were consequently forced to get out of bed and indulge in each of the several times a night he woke up. Dr Richard Ferber, in *Solve Your Child's Sleep Problems,* relates the case of Betsy, a ten-month-old baby.

In the evening Betsy's mother or father had to rock her and rub her back until she fell asleep, which usually took twenty minutes. They said that Betsy seemed to be trying to stay awake instead of letting herself fall asleep. She would begin to doze off then would suddenly open her eyes and look around before starting to nod off again. Her parents could not move her into the cot until she had been solidly asleep for fifteen minutes, or she would wake and start crying again. It was difficult to decide when her sleep was deep enough for her to be moved successfully. If her mother or father moved too soon from the rocking chair, she might wake and they would have to start all over again . . . Between midnight and 4.00 am, Betsy would wake several times. Each time she would cry vigorously and would not settle on her own. At these times she did not seem to be in pain, and in fact when her mother or father went in, picked her up and began to rock her, she would quiet promptly and return to sleep quickly . . . On one occasion, at [a] doctor's suggestion, they planned to let her cry until she fell asleep on her own. Betsy just cried harder and harder, and after an hour and a half her parents decided they were being cruel.

I feel a certain warmth for Betsy's parents, if not for Betsy herself. Their story reassures me of the existence, somewhere between the loud ranks of those who claim never or always to have left their children to cry, of a confederacy of vacillators and fools, of which I am a member. The night comes on like a storm over a desolate sea, upon which we sail in an uncaptained ship deploying measures by turns drastic and sentimental. We are heroic and cruel, authoritative and then servile, cleaving to our guesses and inspirations and bizarre rituals in the absence of any real understanding of what we are doing or how it should properly be done. A friend comes to stay overnight, and in the morning puts a slow and disbelieving head around our bedroom door. Since we last saw her, the evening before, we have run marathons, negotiated the Maastricht Treaty, extinguished forest fires. Our daughter now sits on the bed between our broken bodies like some triumphal mini-Napoleon, waving her rattle in victory. The friend has overheard from her room something of our nocturnal adventures, and come away with the – mostly correct – impression that nobody slept at all. You've got to do something, she says. You're making a rod for your own back. A desire to cry and confess, to seek some impartial, therapeutic embrace comes over me. I feel suddenly that I have experienced trauma. For almost a year of nights I have gone to bed as one would go to bed knowing that the front door was wide open, that there was something on the stove, that the alarm clock was set to go off hourly until dawn, with a new method of silencing it to be devised somehow each time. I have gone to bed like other people get up for work, alert, keyed up, and steeled for battle.

I consult Dr Ferber, who assures me that in all his years of practice he has never met a child who couldn't become a champion sleeper, bar those with serious disabilities. I am halted in my reading by thoughts of those disabled children and their parents. Dr Ferber has been wise to mention them so insouciantly. I read on, understanding that I have not experienced trauma, merely inconvenience. Do not sedate your child, continues Dr Ferber; in the end drugs just make the problem worse. I had not, in fact, considered this option. I consider it now. Dr Ferber clearly believes that children's sleep problems are caused by their parents. You'll leave them to cry, he says, but *you won't leave them to go to sleep*. Mentally I swat myself away like some persistent, sleep-depriving fly. I recognise that the sleep battle indeed seems to occur at the furthest frontier of what a particular parent will tolerate. The authors of *My Child Won't Sleep* concur in this theory: a decision by the parents to resolve the problem, they say, usually itself resolves the problem. I begin to imagine my daughter as some curious incubus, a small, fleshly enactment of my own nightmares. I see that I must cast her out of my dreams – but how?

Dr Ferber does not strictly believe in leaving children to cry. Leaving them to cry, he says, results in a lot of crying. I am beginning to find Ferber intriguingly complex. Some crying is inevitable, he adds. At first the baby's expectations are going to be confounded, which will make her cry; but she'll soon see what you're up to. The suggestion is that she'll see what we're up to and go along with it, rather than report us to the authorities. So what *are* we up to, anyway? I am invited to turn to page 74 to review Ferber's timetable. It is composed of columns of figures strictly denoting intervals at which you are permitted briefly to visit your crying baby. My eye wanders to the opposite page, on which there is printed another timetable with columns of figures entitled 'Helping your child learn to stay in bed: Number of minutes to hold the door closed if your child will not stay in bed'. I retreat nervously to the first timetable. Our goal, I am told in a footnote, is to leave the baby in her crib all night without the embellishments of rocking, rubbing, patting, feeding, or, presumably, violent outbursts of rage on my part, while at the same time not giving her the impression that we have gone out, or away on holiday. By briefly visiting her when she cries, says Ferber, you are leading her not to abandon hope, but to make a choice: this choice being that it is preferable to go to sleep than to have someone bursting into your room every seven minutes, staring at you with an expression of dumb tragedy, and then leaving. *My Child Won't Sleep* recommends a similar procedure, which it calls 'checking'. 'Checking' is more parent-oriented than 'visiting', being designed to reassure you that the crying is not caused by physical injury, or by a desperate neighbour climbing through the bedroom window and attempting to murder the baby. But the superior science of 'visiting' lies in the fact that the intervals between visits are gradually lengthened the more the baby cries. The baby is thus kept on a losing wicket. Dr Ferber provides you with a chart to fill in, indicating your child's sleep patterns, to keep you busy while you're waiting.

It's only mid-afternoon, but I fill in the chart immediately in a sudden access of self-pity. It involves shading in squares for those hours during which the baby sleeps, while leaving hours when she is awake and crying blank. By the end the chart resembles a piano keyboard, or a graveyard. Ferber goes on to detail the case of a woman whose husband insisted that she get up to breastfeed their baby several times a night, as it was the only way to get the child back to sleep. The woman soon became disaffected with both the husband and the baby, although she wisely visited Dr Ferber before taking herself and her breasts elsewhere. I am too proud, I realise, to follow Ferber's advice to the letter, but one night I do attempt an approximation of it. My daughter rips off and devours the early intervals between visits in one sneering swallow. Eight minutes? Thirteen? What, she roars, you think I'm chicken? An interval of thirty-five minutes elapses. We lie silently in the darkness, arms folded across our chests, like courtly figures on a tomb. Next door the baby rages, bellows, chokes, appears to stop breathing for minutes at a time. I wonder whether she's actually ill. I am convinced that I can detect a note of suffering in her cries, a plaintive sound amid the solid chords of outrage. I think there's something wrong with her, I say, leaping to my feet. Moments later she is in our bed, slurping baby medicine from a spoon and chortling. The next night we try again. I have hardened my heart. I visit cursorily, coldly, and am blown from the room upon gusts of infant fury. By 2 am she has worked her way through Ferber's timetable and sustained an episode of uninterrupted crying of three and a quarter hours; some way beyond the maximum of which the doctor's scheme conceives. The knowledge that we are now on our own in uncharted territory, territory wherein the good doctor dares not wander, territory populated by chimeras of cruelty, child abuse and perhaps even crying-related brain damage hangs over us. Mysteriously, the crying stops. I strain to listen, and presently hear the softer, paroxysmic sound of sobbing. A feeling of guilt, and of some awful fore-knowledge, propels me into the baby's room, where I find her standing up but apparently asleep, her body pressed against the side of her crib, her fists gripping the bars, her small face crushed into the gap between. A convulsive sob and sigh issues from it. Gently I prise the body loose, lay it down and cover it in blankets, as dolefully as if I were interring it.

I return to bed. The dark house is filled with silence. It is a silence I feel I have purchased brutally, illegally, like a death by contract. I remember reading somewhere that in primitive societies people sleep all together, huddled with their babies in groups; around a fire, perhaps, built to keep the wild animals away. They do not sit outside their children's bedrooms with a stopwatch and a childcare manual at 3 am. I know that in spite of its old associations with poverty and incest, co-sleeping, as it is called, is adhered to with evangelical fervour in some quarters and queen-sizes. In this far-flung region of the night, I guiltily ponder the co-sleeping philosophy. I relive my daughter's cries, now hearing in them a certain justice, as if she had gone to the gallows protesting her innocence. *We're not supposed to sleep all alone in separate rooms!* she pleads. *In primitive societies they sleep together around a lovely fire, with animals!* To doubt the basic proposition of sleep occurring in separate beds in separate rooms is like doubting the honesty of the police, or whether doctors know what they are doing. The world changes colour. A daunting new sphere of effort, decision and judgement is revealed.

Nevertheless I toss and turn, increasingly certain that I have done some terrible wrong. I consider going in and waking her up in order to offer some atonement. An hour or two passes. Presently a noise from the baby's room, at first sporadic, then persistent, threads its way through my tormented ruminations. There is a rustle, a creak, then a thud. Silence. Rustle, creak, thud. Rustle, creak, thud. I hear her voice, not crying but sort of talking. Rustle, creak, thud. Delighted laughter, like someone at a cocktail party. Silently I rise and go in. Through the darkness I can make out a curious shape in the baby's crib, a sort of blanketed pyramid. With a creak it slowly topples over on to its side and lands with a thump on the mattress. More solitary laughter. Beneath the blankets the baby raises her bottom in the air again, balancing on her hands and feet to form a human triangle. Thump, over she goes. I retreat to my room, confused and somewhat afraid. Thus far I have journeyed through a year of nights using only two emotional gears, anger and remorse. This new situation is outside the range of both. She is not crying, nor unhappy, nor in fact demanding anything of me at all; and yet in spite of its self-sufficiency, the bizarreness of her behaviour cannot but provoke and trouble me, while, according to the terms of our sleep war, depriving me of the right to intervene. She appears to have come to an early understanding of the nature of adolescence.

'When a man is asleep,' writes Proust in *Swann's Way*, 'he has in a circle round him the chain of the hours, the sequence of the years, the order of the heavenly bodies.' Is it possible so to violate the geography of one's being that it is no longer possible to locate oneself on the map of time? Not to sleep is not to let your creation rest, to be trapped in an ever-spreading sphere of activity. And yet what is the sleep that I remember, the sleep of the past, but an old-fashioned idyll, like an Alpine village? Perhaps it never even existed, in spite of my possession by the notion of finding it once more, my certain memory of the savour of its empty hours. Without it the refugeless night is long and bleak, as compassionless as a mountain; or busy and built-up, with a headachy neon glare, like a motorway service station that is open all hours. I used to dream of my own homecoming to sleep; now I dream of my daughter's. It is as if I have given up hope of it, or fear that I will be disappointed by it, and in any case it seems to have become a haunted place for me. I am woken now by the ghosts of her cries, keeping their old hours. Sometimes, if I lie awake long enough she will wake too and cry, as if I gave her the idea. Usually, I suspect that I did. Most nights, anyway, I still get up for her at least once; while by those other, silent, wakings I am retained, like some faithful old-timer with nowhere else to go, allowed to keep his habits where once he toiled. I would like my daughter to sleep. For myself, I'll just wait for morning. 'I would strike a match to look at my watch,' continues Proust:

> Nearly midnight. The hour when an invalid, who has been obliged to set out on a journey and to sleep in a strange hotel, awakened by a sudden spasm, sees with glad relief a streak of daylight showing under his door. 'Thank God, it is morning!' The servants will be about in a minute: he can ring, and someone will come to look after him. The thought of being assuaged gives him strength to endure his pain. He is certain he heard footsteps: they come nearer, and then die away. The ray of light beneath his door is extinguished. It is midnight; someone has just turned down the gas; the last servant has gone to bed, and he must lie all night suffering without remedy.

Breathe

My friend Miranda told me that at night she lies awake listening to her baby breathe. Miranda's baby, Alexander, is three weeks older than mine. He has a large white head and a small face with precise features. His forehead is enormous, like a great sea on a globe banking away from the detail of his eyebrows, meeting the North Pole of his cap of fine hair. He is voluble and his gesturing arms fly about, as if he were conversing enthusiastically in a language I don't understand. When Miranda and I were pregnant I thought that we were in it together, that we were somehow doing it together, but in fact it hasn't turned out like that. When I spoke to her after Alexander was born I knew straight away that it wasn't going to be like that. After the conspiracy of pregnancy, having the baby amounts almost to a betrayal. Her husband called her to the phone and she took such a long time to come that it was clear she had gone somewhere far away, alone, and come back altered. I didn't know, I thought maybe that was just what happened. She told me all about the birth, about the baby, in the same way I sensed she was telling everybody about it. So how are *you*? she said at the end. The way she said it made me feel uncomfortable, like someone she was taking pity on standing on their own at a party. It was like she had been elected to something, chosen above me. Anyway, I still phone her most weeks, whether I think she wants me to or not. The stark bond of our common predicament is enough for me. Like immigrants from the same tiny, distant island, it seems to me that we're stuck with each other.

When she said it I almost asked why, so strange at first did the idea seem to me of listening to Alexander breathe. At night I sometimes put my pillow over my head to block out my own baby's sounds, the tortuous narrative of her breath, the strange hoots and squeaks that people her nocturnal life, the pauses. I can't sleep otherwise. For some reason I imagine Alexander's breath to be more regular, the vigorous in-out in-out of bellows, Miranda alert as a hospital monitor next to him in the dark, ready to go off like an alarm if the breathing stops. I didn't mean to find her concern ridiculous. It's just that my own was so raw and rude and new, so engulfing. Alexander's shape and smell, his being, did not trigger my love. I could only understand Miranda's vigilance by translating it into my own maternal tongue.

She said that she lay awake hour after hour, logging his breaths, amassing them, and that it was only when he began to wake up, stuttering into life with the ignition of hunger, that correspondingly, finally, having guided him through the death-parallax of sleep, she could be submerged in it herself. This was inconvenient, given that this was also the moment at which she had to get up and feed him. A vista of her life opened out before me, plunging and dramatic and untraversable. I had imagined that no one could be as tired as I, as bruised by the violence done to their nights. But when do you sleep? I asked. Ah, *sleep*, she said in a funny voice. Sleep is over. Sleep is as far out of fashion as shoulder-pads. She said this on the phone so I couldn't see her face. I wondered what she looked like, and whether what she was saying was true. I wondered if her particularly groomed beauty was in disarray. People told me I looked fine, but I felt interrupted, bugged, like an invaded microchip.

What do you think is going to happen, I said, that he's just going to stop breathing? I had heard of people rushing day and night to their babies' cribs to check they were still alive, but I had never felt the urge to do it myself. I took my daughter's sleep forcibly, like a gift I wanted but the giver was prevaricating in handing over. I know it's silly, Miranda said; and I imagined these other people would say exactly the same thing, but it still added up to make me feel that I lacked something, some importance, some force of presumption. I did not think to investigate the bureaucracy of breathing. I laboured under it and expected my child to labour too. Well, I said, he's got to be able to breathe. He's got to be able to do that for himself. The way I said it reminded me of someone crushing and conservative, someone I didn't like. I know, said Miranda. Then she admitted that she'd read a book about babies who died in their sleep, who just stopped like unwound clocks, for no reason anyone could discover, and now she couldn't think about anything else.

This admission didn't, in fact, surprise me. It merely gave substance to a feeling I'd had about Miranda all these weeks, that she was like something out of a book, a textbook, a manual, the kind of book I had begun to read since having a baby had provided me, for the first time, with an experience that was apparently normal and yet entirely unintelligible. Anyway, everything it said in these books, Miranda seemed to feel. Her life was in agreement with them where mine was not. The things she said increasingly merged in my mind with the so-called mothers' comments these books are full of. *I had expected to need drugs in my labour, but when it came to it the breathing exercises I'd learned in antenatal classes were enough.* Or, *Breastfeeding was a little tricky at first, but then we both came to love it!* Or, *Making love was a little tricky at first, but once we'd got the hang of it, it was even better than before!* There was something even about Miranda's vulnerability, her fear that struck me as official and endorsed, where my own anxieties shrank from the light, dreading disclosure. Still, I'd read enough to keep me in the conversation, and others like it.

That's not going to happen to Alexander, I said. I know, said Miranda. It's very, very rare, I said. I *know,* wailed Miranda, I just can't get the image out of my head! It turned out that this book she'd read was written by a woman who had found her four-month-old son dead in his crib one morning. The 'image' was in fact many images: of the summer beauty of the morning she found him, of his stiff little body rising entire from the mattress when she lifted his arm, of his bottle of milk found still curdling in the warming pan hours later, when his death had become a fact and his life a memory. Of course, Miranda said, that baby was left to sleep face-down in a room on his own on a hot night. And he was bottle-fed, she added. What's that got to do with it? I said. Well, they now think that breastfeeding offers some protection against crib death, she said. I mentioned that my daughter slept face-down, her legs curled beneath her, her cheek pressed against the rotating earth; the clinging, elemental posture of something growing. Does she, said Miranda. Her voice was surprised and polite.

Not long after that conversation, Miranda came with Alexander to see me. Or perhaps it wasn't to see me: perhaps she came because she had to, because I had made the journey to her house with my daughter several times while she had never once visited me, because in spite of her silence I continued to phone her, to ask her to come. So finally, one day, she came, and when she arrived full of relief and pride at having taken the bus all the way across town without incident, without Alexander having cried or dirtied his nappy or gone off like a bomb in a public place as she seemed to expect him to, I saw that it was not that she disdained my company, but that she was afraid; of the city, of its noise and poisonous air and danger, of stepping out into its unpredictability; and of Alexander, of what he might do once moved outside the limits of her house, her control, the known world of her care of him. I saw that her mastery of him was glancing and rudimentary. Like a complex piece of equipment in whose use she was untrained, he responded to certain things she did without her really knowing why, and so she adhered to those things and dared try nothing else. The truth was that I felt the same fear of my own baby, but in me it provoked a certain violence, made me embark with her on long journeys by tube or train, take her on camping trips or to parties. I was always miserable at these times, rigid with responsibility and worry, so full of anticipation that I forgot to breathe. My head would begin to hurt and an ache would creep across my chest, and then I would remember and take great scalding gulps of air that sluiced over my parched lungs and made my throat burn. It was as if at these times I just stopped living because I was so taken up with looking after someone else.

Alexander whined and grizzled the whole afternoon. Miranda said it was because he was teething, because he needed his nap, because he was in a strange place. It didn't matter to me. She plugged and unplugged him raging from her breast, his limbs flailing, his clothes riding up uncomfortably around his plump little body. Milk tipped from his mouth as they wrestled and spilled over her clothes, and she scrubbed at it with his knitted hat. Don't use that, I said, I'll get a cloth. I offered to hold him, wanting her to relax, and she gave him to me as if she had to, for the sake of politeness. He was unfamiliar, much heavier than my daughter and different-smelling. His unco-ordinated body was strong and muscled and frantic with tension. Grappling with him was like trying to rescue someone who was drowning. I was so used to holding my daughter that it felt like a sort of infidelity. We talked while all this was going on. Everything I said Miranda agreed with, meekly, which just made me talk more. I talked about how difficult it all was, about the anarchy of nights, the fog of days, about friendlessness and exile from the past and exclusion, about the wordless tyranny of babies and the strange, obsessive task of being alone with them all day, about my feelings of claustrophobia, my feeling that I was shut in a box, that I couldn't breathe. That's right, that's right, Miranda would say, nodding her head distantly. It got to the point where I thought she wasn't listening, until just then she spoke. But it's great as well, she said. You mustn't forget all the good things. She said it quite firmly, but for a minute I really didn't know what she was talking about. It was as if I was reading one of those books again. I almost said, there aren't any good things. She had Alexander back by this time and he was quiet because she was feeding him again. I wondered if she had said it because she thought she ought to. I wanted to ask her what the good things were. She went home saying she'd had a really nice time, that it was a real achievement to have got out of the house, and I believed her.

One day, in the bookshop, I found that book Miranda had talked about. My daughter was asleep in her stroller, so I parked it up by the bookshelf and began to read there in the shop. I read quickly, skimming over chapters, plunging in where I sensed something important was occurring. There were photos and I lingered over those. The baby who'd died looked older than I had expected, more robust. I couldn't believe he'd died. I couldn't believe Miranda had actually bought so ghoulish, so sentimental a book either. When I got to the morning on which she found him, tears surged powerfully and painfully to my eyes. I rubbed at them behind my glasses. The author described holding the stiff little body with its cruciform arms, and I wanted to pick up my sleeping daughter and hold her too. I realised then that I could have her for ever, could keep her, and the thought engulfed me in uncontrollable feeling, in the ferment of love. At the end of the book the author describes going on holiday with her family – later, when it was all over – to a place she had last been to when the baby was alive. Getting up one morning she puts on a sundress, a dress she hasn't worn since that last time. In the pocket she finds one of the baby's tiny socks; and she smells it and it smells of him, and she cries and cries.

Heartburn

My daughter fell and cut her head on a sharp stone, and when I picked her up to comfort her she fought to escape my arms, her face a panicked blur of tears and mucus. She wanted her father; frantically, blindly, she wanted to get away from me. Even in the heat of her injury I felt my own more keenly. I remain surprised by how proximate the mythology of motherhood is to its reality. I needed to be her mother more than she needed my mothering. The perfect regard with which I wanted to arm my daughter is still joined to me and I cannot cut the cord. I see that my desire for her sufficiency is in fact my own, my own desire to be sufficient to another, and it remains thwarted. *You came from my body!* I wanted to say. I was offering her what I had craved often in my life, another body in which to be absorbed, enfolded, enclosed, an element in which to be reincorporated, and she didn't want it. In this moment a vista of the future was lit up, a brief vision illuminated as if by lightening. In this vision I could see myself feeling exactly the same thing ten, twenty, thirty years hence, unanaesthetised by time or custom.

I miss my daughter's babyhood already. In her growing up I have watched the present become the past, have seen at first hand how life acquires the savour of longing. The storm of emotion, of the new, that accompanied her arrival is over now. I find that I am living in the knowledge of what I have, so that I see happiness before it quite passes. It has taken me a year to achieve this feat, this skill that has eluded me over a lifetime. I understand that it means that I am standing still. Motherhood sometimes seems to me like a sort of relay race, a journey whose purpose is to pass on the baton of life, all work and heat and hurry one minute and mere panting spectatorship the next; a team enterprise in which stardom is endlessly reconfigured, transferred. I see my daughter hurrying away from me, hurtling towards her future, and in that sight I recognise my ending, my frontier, the boundary of my life.

Mothers are the countries we come from: sometimes when I hold my daughter I try to apprehend this belonging for her, to feel myself as solid and fixed, to capture my smell and shape and atmosphere. I try to flesh out her native landscape. I try to imagine what it would be like to have me as a mother, and when I do it seems remarkable to me that this mysterious and momentous transaction has been accomplished here, in my house. The transaction I refer to is not that which has brought my daughter into existence: it is the process by which a mother has been made of me, and though I know it is the hardest work I have ever done I still worry that my execution of it has been somehow flawed and unauthentic, a burned offering, a botched canvas. Perhaps it is only children who confer upon their parents this meaning I feel myself to lack. I don't think it is. I think, rather, that there is some conservatism inherent in the constitution of families, that it is parents who inflict on their children the onerous culture of leadership, so that like politicians they conform once they themselves are in power, living out their childish fear of authority by assuming its harsh and dreary mantle. Their resolutions forgotten, they become that against which they used to rail and protest. They find respect for those they hated. They feel a marvellous, secret sense of peace when the same words come out of their mouths that used to anger them so. I often hear people say that they really understand their parents now that they have become parents themselves, and the sentiment fills me with unease and foreboding, with the sense of some wrong being passed down the generations like a disease. It makes me want to tolerate my daughter until I am negated, so that there can be no years lost to mis-understanding. I vow to own my feelings of inadequacy and inauthenticity. I vow to end this succession, this history of ruler and ruled, here, with me.

Brief pauses begin to appear in the score of motherhood, silences like the silences between album tracks, surrounded by sound but silences nontheless. In them I begin to glimpse myself, briefly, like someone walking past my window. The sight is a shock, like the sight of someone thought dead. As my daughter grows more separate from me, so the silences become longer, the glimpses more sustained. I realise that I had accepted each stage of her dependence on me as a new and permanent reality, as if I were living in a house whose rooms were being painted and forgot that I had ever had the luxury of their use. First one room and then another is given back to me. Stairs are just stairs again. Nights are once more vague and soundless. Time is no longer alarmed and trip-wired: things can wait, can be explained and deferred. My body has lost its memory of her birth and sometimes I feel surges of girlishness, of youth and lightness.

My daughter has realised that I am different from her. She offers me her lunch and tickles my feet. She makes me laugh. I find things in my pockets, in my shoes, leaves and shells, half-eaten biscuits, a doll's tiny plastic handbag, things she has put there like small offerings to an unimportant goddess. When I return from an absence she runs all the way down the passage and throws herself into my arms. I pick her up and hug her like something I had thought lost. Once, when I am upset and want to stay at home while everyone else goes for a walk, I see her standing at the door in her red coat, her face filled with anxiety. She gets my boots and brings them to where I sit. Another adult picks her up and carries her outside without noticing what she has done, and as the door shuts behind them I am left with the boots, the expression of her love, sitting neatly side by side on the kitchen floor.

Increasingly, motherhood comes to seem to me not a condition but a job, the work of certain periods, which begin and end and outside of which I am free. My daughter is more and more a part of this freedom, something new that is being added, drop by daily drop, to the sum of what I am. We are an admixture, an experiment. I don't yet know what effect her presence will have on my life, but its claim is more profound, more unnerving than was the mere work of looking after her. For the first year of her life work and love were bound together, fiercely, painfully. Now, it is as if a relationship has untethered itself and been let loose in our house. A storm of association rages around her, and at first I find this change relieving, as if I had been speaking a foreign language all this time and could at last revert to my native tongue. But in fact, she has not been waiting all this time merely to speak to me: her ability to relate to other people has grown, like tentacles, out of the body of what she has already become. When finally we are able to converse, I find her decided, fully formed, already beyond the reach of persuasion. My relationship with her is like my relationship with anybody: it takes the form of a search for oneness, a oneness lost but haunting with the prospect of its recapture. It is incredible to me – who remembers that oneness, the image on the snowy screen of her two-inch-long body lying in my darkness, as if it were yesterday, as if it were still there – that our joinedness is for her such a distant state. Sitting on the sofa with her watching cartoons, I put an arm around her and she shakes it irritably off. Minutes later she places a small, plump hand consolingly on my knee. Neither of us says anything. We are like awkward lovers, like two people, any old people, clumsily sharing the regular cup of human emotion. In such moments I feel as though I have survived what insurance policies refer to as an act of God, a hurricane, a flood. It roared around me threatening destruction and then vanished, leaving silence and a world strewn with broken things, a world I patiently repair, wondering what I can salvage, whether I'd be better off just starting again.

I go to London, alone, for the weekend and walk stupidly around Oxford Street in the glare of an urban summer. Everything seems weirdly futuristic, as if I had been deposited there by a time machine. I want to buy clothes, to make up for two years in which I have been as far from fashion as an anthropologist on a long field trip; but the racks of things look incomprehensible and unrelated to me, like costumes for a drama in which I no longer have a part. I lack the desire for myself that would teach me what to choose; I lack the sense of stardom in my own life that would urge me to adorn myself. I am backstage, attendant. I have the curious feeling that I no longer exist in synchronicity with time, but at a certain delay, like some-one on the end of a transatlantic phone call. This, I think, is what it is to be a mother. The most terrible feeling of stress and anxiety begins to mount in me there in the shop. My heart flails in my chest with panic. I long for my child, long for her as for a sort of double, a tiny pilot boat winging young and certain up the channel ahead of me, guiding the blind, clumsy weight of me through. I go to the children's section of a department store and stand there amidst the cribs and the baby clothes, the teddy bears and tiny shoes, and I feel alleviated, rescued, plugged into a source of life.

All day I have heard babies crying, faint threads of distress from elsewhere borne past me on the air, and each time I have felt a fine quiver of response, razor-sharp, immediate, and have had to steel myself not to look around. A baby begins to cry there in the children's department, not six feet away from me. It is the raw, tiny cry of someone only a few days old. I look up and see the stroller, the mother frantically jiggling it with one hand while raking through racks of baby clothes with the other, her face a fist of concentration. She is debating something in urgent tones with the older woman – her mother – standing next to her. The baby's cries are fast with barely a beat between them. I know that this means the woman has less than a minute to choose and purchase an outfit, but her mother disagrees with her choice and is remonstrating with her. I can see by the way she moves that her body is still stunned with childbirth. Go home, I think. Go home. Wrap the baby in a tea-towel, she won't care. Just give in and go home. She doesn't give in. She has an image of this shopping expedition and she is clinging to it with sharp teeth. She can't bear something to go unresolved, unfinished, for she fears that nothing will ever be resolved again. She's trying to keep up, to stay in time, but she's swimming against a powerful current. I see her steal looks at her mother, brimming with longing and confusion and hurt. After all these years she has discovered her mother's secret and it is somehow disppointing, a let-down, for she is in those first days of her parturition both mother and child, and the passionate emotion she feels for her vulnerable self finds no reflection in her own mother's disapproval, her compassionless urge to dispute. Years of human politics have adhered to her mother's heart: they hang from it like stalectites, like moss. Her own heart is new, raw, frantically pulsing. Will time turn it, too, unfeeling?

The baby cries and cries; and it is all I can do not to lift it from its stroller and hold its small, frightened body close against my chest, hold it and hold it until it stops, so certain am I that it would, that it would know that I knew, and be consoled.

Credits

Extract from 'The Bad Mother' by James Hillman featured in *Fathers and Mothers* ed. P. Berry (Spring Publications 1990)

Extract from *The Great Fortune* by Olivia Manning © Olivia Manning 1960 (Arrow 2000)

Extract from *Of Woman Born* by Adrienne Rich, published by Virago Press

Extract from *Solve Your Child's Sleep Problems* by Dr Richard Ferber © Dr Richard Ferber (Dorling Kindersley 1986)